THE
QUAPAWS

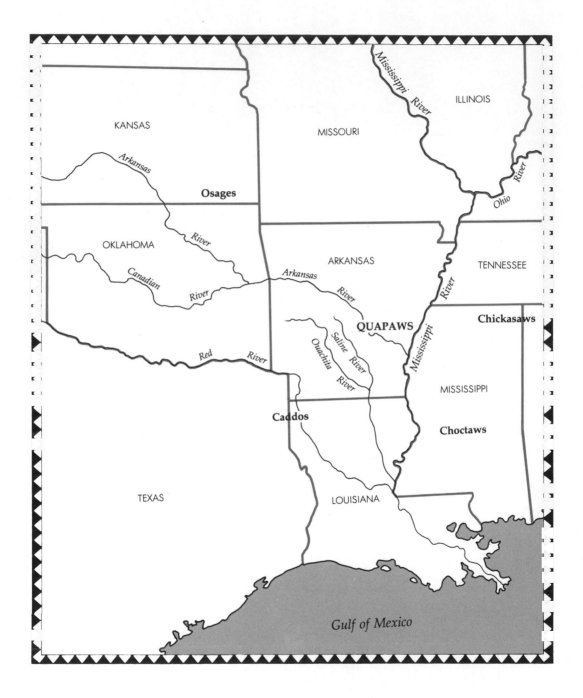

THE
QUAPAWS

W. David Baird
Pepperdine University

Frank W. Porter III
General Editor

CHELSEA HOUSE PUBLISHERS
New York   Philadelphia

On the cover A Quapaw clay teapot in the shape of a fawn

Chelsea House Publishers
Editor-in-Chief Nancy Toff
Executive Editor Remmel T. Nunn
Managing Editor Karyn Gullen Browne
Copy Chief Juliann Barbato
Picture Editor Adrian G. Allen
Art Director Maria Epes
Manufacturing Manager Gerald Levine

Indians of North America
Senior Editor Marjorie P. K. Weiser

Staff for **THE QUAPAWS**
Associate Editor Liz Sonneborn
Deputy Copy Chief Ellen Scordato
Editorial Assistant Claire M. Wilson
Assistant Art Director Laurie Jewell
Designer Donna Sinisgalli
Design Assistant James Baker
Layout Victoria Tomaselli
Picture Researchers Kim Dramer and Kathryn Bonomi
Production Coordinator Joseph Romano

First Printing

1 3 5 7 9 8 6 4 2

Library of Congress Cataloging-in-Publication Data

Baird, W. David.
The Quapaw / W. David Baird.
p. cm.—(Indians of North America)
Bibliography: p.
Includes index.
ISBN 1-55546-728-8.   ISBN 0-7910-0397-3 (pbk.)
1. Quapaw Indians. I. Title. II. Series: Indians of North
America (Chelsea House Publishers)
E99.Q2B32 1989   88-25943
970'.004'97—dc 19   CIP

CONTENTS

INDIANS OF NORTH AMERICA

CHELSEA HOUSE PUBLISHERS

INDIANS OF NORTH AMERICA: CONFLICT AND SURVIVAL

Frank W. Porter III

*The Indians survived our
open intention of wiping them
out, and since the tide turned
they have even weathered
our good intentions toward them,
which can be much more deadly.*

John Steinbeck
America and Americans

When Europeans first reached the North American continent, they found hundreds of tribes occupying a vast and rich country. The newcomers quickly recognized the wealth of natural resources. They were not, however, so quick or willing to recognize the spiritual, cultural, and intellectual riches of the people they called Indians.

The Indians of North America examines the problems that develop when people with different cultures come together. For American Indians, the consequences of their interaction with non-Indian people have been both productive and tragic. The Europeans believed they had "discovered" a "New World," but their religious bigotry, cultural bias, and materialistic world view kept them from appreciating and understanding the people who lived in it. All too often they attempted to change the way of life of the indigenous people. The Spanish conquistadores wanted the Indians as a source of labor. The Christian missionaries, many of whom were English, viewed them as potential converts. French traders and trappers used the Indians as a means to obtain pelts. As Francis Parkman, the 19th-century historian, stated, "Spanish civilization crushed the Indian; English civilization scorned and neglected him; French civilization embraced and cherished him."

Nearly 500 years later, many people think of American Indians as curious vestiges of a distant past, waging a futile war to survive in a Space Age society. Even today, our understanding of the history and culture of American Indians is too often derived from unsympathetic, culturally biased, and inaccurate reports. The American Indian, described and portrayed in thousands of movies, television programs, books, articles, and government studies, has either been raised to the status of the "noble savage" or disparaged as the "wild Indian" who resisted the westward expansion of the American frontier.

Where in this popular view are the real Indians, the human beings and communities whose ancestors can be traced back to ice-age hunters? Where are the creative and indomitable people whose sophisticated technologies used the natural resources to ensure their survival, whose military skill might even have prevented European settlement of North America if not for devastating epidemics and the disruption of the ecology? Where are the men and women who are today diligently struggling to assert their legal rights and express once again the value of their heritage?

The various Indian tribes of North America, like people everywhere, have a history that includes population expansion, adaptation to a range of regional environments, trade across wide networks, internal strife, and warfare. This was the reality. Europeans justified their conquests, however, by creating a mythical image of the New World and its native people. In this myth, the New World was a virgin land, waiting for the Europeans. The arrival of Christopher Columbus ended a timeless primitiveness for the original inhabitants.

Also part of this myth was the debate over the origins of the American Indians. Fantastic and diverse answers were proposed by the early explorers, missionaries, and settlers. Some thought that the Indians were descended from the Ten Lost Tribes of Israel, others that they were descended from inhabitants of the lost continent of Atlantis. One writer suggested that the Indians had reached North America in another Noah's ark.

A later myth, perpetrated by many historians, focused on the relentless persecution during the past five centuries until only a scattering of these "primitive" people remained to be herded onto reservations. This view fails to chronicle the overt and covert ways in which the Indians successfully coped with the intruders.

All of these myths presented one-sided interpretations that ignored the complexity of European and American events and policies. All left serious questions unanswered. What were the origins of the American Indians? Where did they come from? How and when did they get to the New World? What was their life—their culture—really like?

In the late 1800s, anthropologists and archaeologists in the Smithsonian Institution's newly created Bureau of American Ethnology in Washington, D. C., began to study scientifically the history and culture of the Indians of North America. They were motivated by an honest belief that the Indians were on the verge of extinction and that along with them would vanish their languages, religious beliefs, technology, myths, and legends. These men and women went out to visit, study, and record data from as many Indian communities as possible before this information was forever lost.

By this time there was a new myth in the national consciousness. American Indians existed as figures in the American past. They had performed a historical mission. They had challenged white settlers who trekked across the continent. Once conquered, however, they were supposed to accept graciously the way of life of their conquerors.

The reality again was different. American Indians resisted both actively and passively. They refused to lose their unique identity, to be assimilated into white society. Many whites viewed the Indians not only as members of a conquered nation but also as "inferior" and "unequal." The rights of the Indians could be expanded, contracted, or modified as the conquerors saw fit. In every generation, white society asked itself what to do with the American Indians. Their answers have resulted in the twists and turns of federal Indian policy.

There were two general approaches. One way was to raise the Indians to a "higher level" by "civilizing" them. Zealous missionaries considered it their Christian duty to elevate the Indian through conversion and scanty education. The other approach was to ignore the Indians until they disappeared under pressure from the ever-expanding white society. The myth of the "vanishing Indian" gave stronger support to the latter option, helping to justify the taking of the Indians' land.

Prior to the end of the 18th century, there was no national policy on Indians simply because the American nation had not yet come into existence. American Indians similarly did not possess a political or social unity with which to confront the various Europeans. They were not homogeneous. Rather, they were loosely formed bands and tribes, speaking nearly 300 languages and thousands of dialects. The collective identity felt by Indians today is a result of their common experiences of defeat and/or mistreatment at the hands of whites.

During the colonial period, the British crown did not have a coordinated policy toward the Indians of North America. Specific tribes (most notably the Iroquois and the Cherokee) became military and political pawns used by both the crown and the individual colonies. The success of the American Revolution brought no immediate change. When the United States acquired new territory from France and Mexico in the early 19th century, the federal government wanted to open this land to settlement by homesteaders. But the Indian tribes that lived on this land had signed treaties with European governments assuring their title to the land. Now the United States assumed legal responsibility for honoring these treaties.

At first, President Thomas Jefferson believed that the Louisiana Purchase contained sufficient land for both the Indians and the white population.

9

Within a generation, though, it became clear that the Indians would not be allowed to remain. In the 1830s the federal government began to coerce the eastern tribes to sign treaties agreeing to relinquish their ancestral land and move west of the Mississippi River. Whenever these negotiations failed, President Andrew Jackson used the military to remove the Indians. The southeastern tribes, promised food and transportation during their removal to the West, were instead forced to walk the "Trail of Tears." More than 4,000 men, women, and children died during this forced march. The "removal policy" was successful in opening the land to homesteaders, but it created enormous hardships for the Indians.

By 1871 most of the tribes in the United States had signed treaties ceding most or all of their ancestral land in exchange for reservations and welfare. The treaty terms were intended to bind both parties for all time. But in the General Allotment Act of 1887, the federal government changed its policy again. Now the goal was to make tribal members into individual landowners and farmers, encouraging their absorption into white society. This policy was advantageous to whites who were eager to acquire Indian land, but it proved disastrous for the Indians. One hundred thirty-eight million acres of reservation land were subdivided into tracts of 160, 80, or as little as 40 acres, and allotted to tribe members on an individual basis. Land owned in this way was said to have "trust status" and could not be sold. But the surplus land—all Indian land not allotted to individuals— was opened (for sale) to white settlers. Ultimately, more than 90 million acres of land were taken from the Indians by legal and illegal means.

The resulting loss of land was a catastrophe for the Indians. It was necessary to make it illegal for Indians to sell their land to non-Indians. The Indian Reorganization Act of 1934 officially ended the allotment period. Tribes that voted to accept the provisions of this act were reorganized, and an effort was made to purchase land within preexisting reservations to restore an adequate land base.

Ten years later, in 1944, federal Indian policy again shifted. Now the federal government wanted to get out of the "Indian business." In 1953 an act of Congress named specific tribes whose trust status was to be ended "at the earliest possible time." This new law enabled the United States to end unilaterally, whether the Indians wished it or not, the special status that protected the land in Indian tribal reservations. In the 1950s federal Indian policy was to transfer federal responsibility and jurisdiction to state governments, encourage the physical relocation of Indian peoples from reservations to urban areas, and hasten the termination, or extinction, of tribes.

10

Between 1954 and 1962 Congress passed specific laws authorizing the termination of more than 100 tribal groups. The stated purpose of the termination policy was to ensure the full and complete integration of Indians into American society. However, there is a less benign way to interpret this legislation. Even as termination was being discussed in Congress, 133 separate bills were introduced to permit the transfer of trust land ownership from Indians to non-Indians.

With the Johnson administration in the 1960s the federal government began to reject termination. In the 1970s yet another Indian policy emerged. Known as "self-determination," it favored keeping the protective role of the federal government while increasing tribal participation in, and control of, important areas of local government. In 1983 President Reagan, in a policy statement on Indian affairs, restated the unique "government to government" relationship of the United States with the Indians. However, federal programs since then have moved toward transferring Indian affairs to individual states, which have long desired to gain control of Indian land and resources.

As long as American Indians retain power, land, and resources that are coveted by the states and the federal government, there will continue to be a "clash of cultures," and the issues will be contested in the courts, Congress, the White House, and even in the international human rights community. To give all Americans a greater comprehension of the issues and conflicts involving American Indians today is a major goal of this series. These issues are not easily understood, nor can these conflicts be readily resolved. The study of North American Indian history and culture is a necessary and important step toward that comprehension. All Americans must learn the history of the relations between the Indians and the federal government, recognize the unique legal status of the Indians, and understand the heritage and cultures of the Indians of North America.

Every year on July 4, the Quapaw Indians gather for their powwow.
In this festive atmosphere, they reaffirm and celebrate their heritage.

A
SELF-SUFFICIENT
PEOPLE

On July 4, 1988, adults and children filled an air-conditioned hall near Miami, Oklahoma. Called to order by Chairman Harry Gilmore, the group heard reports on government contracts and various business ventures, discussed management policies of the local bingo contractor, voted against a proposed state road, and elected a new set of leaders. The meeting resembled one attended by the stockholders of any other corporation.

That evening, gentle winds cooled a nearby natural amphitheater, which could seat several thousand. Around it were hundreds of campsites—some permanent, some temporary—where family and friends finished meals of corn, meat, fry bread, and grape dumplings. At dusk, measured drumbeats could be heard briefly in the arena. Thirty minutes later the drumming resumed. Dressed in their finest costumes, a line of dancers—first the elders, then the men, and finally the women—snaked rhythmically into the amphitheater, filling it with circles of color in motion. The drummers drummed and the dancers danced

throughout the night. By morning both the dancers and their audience had reaffirmed and celebrated their unique common heritage.

These people—the stockholders and the dancers whose ways seem at once so modern and so ancient—were Quapaws. They are members of a tribe of North American Indians who were once sovereigns of the region where the Arkansas River enters the Mississippi. At different periods in their history, the Quapaws had been powerful allies of France, Spain, and the United States. In 1824, they were forced to abandon their ancestral home and move first to northwestern Louisiana and then, 10 years later, to a reservation in northeastern Oklahoma. Over the next 150 years, the tribe experienced times of poverty and disintegration as well as wealth and renewal. The drums of the Fourth of July powwow, held on a remnant of the tribal reserve, recalled this heritage; the annual business meeting of the tribe pointed to its future.

For the Quapaws, there is no future without a past. They are always aware of being a people of great antiquity, al-

A 17th-century Quapaw, painted by the contemporary Oklahoma artist Charles Banks Wilson. The model who posed for this painting is of Quapaw descent.

though much of their distant past, their prehistory, is cloaked in mystery. Tales passed on orally for generations recall that the Quapaws once lived in the Ohio River valley along with the Osages, Poncas, Kansas, and Omahas. These groups shared many cultural characteristics and spoke similar languages. Driven out of this area by the aggressive Iroquois, these tribes migrated west toward the Mississippi River, probably during the late 16th century. The Osages crossed the river in boats made of animal hides, but the onset of a heavy mist prevented others

from following. The Omahas turned north and crossed the Mississippi upstream. The Quapaws chose to go south to the Arkansas River. Thereafter their kinsmen called the tribe the Ugaxpa, or "those who drifted downstream." The writings of 17th-century European explorers suggest that the Downstream People had to battle other tribes for their new homeland. They forced out the previous occupants, such as the Michigameas and the Tunicas, and often moved into the villages of those they had driven away.

Much more is known about the Quapaw people, their society, and their culture after their migration into the lower Arkansas River valley. Early French explorers, for instance, wrote about their impressive personal appearance. One judged them "the best formed Savages" he had seen, whereas another described them as "the largest and handsomest of all of the Indians of this continent" and worthy of the description *les beaux hommes*, "the handsome men."

The gentle climate of their new homeland allowed the Quapaws to wear little clothing. Wrapped only in deerskins that reached from their waist to their knees, the women were described by the French as "half-naked." The men were usually "stark naked," wearing buffalo robes only during winter months. Europeans later influenced the Quapaws to cover themselves with garments worn by Indians elsewhere—moccasins, leggings, loincloths, and seamed hunting shirts.

The Quapaws' hairstyles and ornaments were more elaborate than their clothing. Men plucked their body hair and shaved the hair on their head, except for a narrow tuft down the center called a scalp lock. They often wore rings, feathers, and beads in their scalp locks and hung beaded pendants on their ears and nose. Unmarried women braided their hair into two plaits, which they wrapped into buns at their ears and ornamented. Married women wore their hair unadorned in a single loose lock.

For ceremonies, the Quapaws decorated their body in a number of ways. Often they wore red and black body paint made from clay and soot or headgear with different-colored feathers, buffalo horns, or caps of deer or rabbit skin. Distinguished warriors in the personal service of the chief also attached gourds filled with pebbles to their waist and the tails of horses or wildcats to

Buffalo was the most important game hunted by the Quapaws. They sometimes traveled as far west as the Wichita Mountains in what is now southwestern Oklahoma in search of buffalo herds.

their backsides. When men danced at ceremonies, they sometimes held gigantic wooden masks before their face. For fertility dances, men often wore a female costume with a head of wood and a hollow leather body.

The Quapaws' new homeland helped them create a self-sufficient economy, because the environment provided a variety of food. From the rivers they took fish and turtles; in the forests they gathered roots, nuts, and berries; in the brush and on the scattered prairies they hunted a variety of

Quapaw women made pottery for their own use and traded it to other Indian tribes as well. The swirling pattern on this example was a favorite design. The Quapaws sometimes painted similar designs on their bodies, as shown in the portrait of a tribesman reproduced on page 14.

game, especially wild birds, deer, and bison (buffalo).

Most of their food, however, came from farming the fertile fields, which were annually renewed by the flooding of the Mississippi and Arkansas rivers. Corn was their most important vegetable crop, although they also grew gourds, pumpkins, sunflowers, beans, and squash. They farmed these crops in large common fields, one of which was estimated in 1682 as measuring eight-and-a-half square miles. By this date, the Quapaws were also cultivating different varieties of fruits, including peaches and watermelons. Because these plants are not native to the Americas, they probably had been carried by Spanish settlers to what are today Florida and New Mexico and introduced to the lower Arkansas River valley before the arrival of the Downstream People.

The presence of European plants is evidence of the vital trade network that linked the Quapaws to other settlements along the Arkansas River. The Quapaws traded their pottery, wooden platters, and canoes to tribes to the east and west for knives, hatchets, and beads—all goods supplied by the Spanish in what are now Florida and New Mexico. With the Caddo Indians on Red River, the Downstream People exchanged their goods for salt and bows and arrows. This commerce also extended up the Mississippi River, which gave the tribe easy access to trading partners to the north who possessed French goods.

Whereas fishing, gathering, hunting, agriculture, and an extensive trading network provided the Quapaws with a productive and stable economy, their political and social customs ordered and gave meaning to their life. The basic unit of the tribal structure was the family. Each family belonged to a clan, a group of relatives who shared property and believed that they were the descendants of a common ancestor. Each of the Quapaws' clans and sub-clans was named for an animal or a cosmic phenomenon, such as Buffalo, Fish, Eagle, Star, Thunder, or Sun. The Quapaws organized their clans into two major divisions, or moieties, known as *Hanka* and, probably, *Tiju*.

The clan system gave the Quapaws a profound sense of identity and social responsibility, as it did for many North American Indian tribes. They felt morally obligated to help and protect other clan members in times of crisis. The system may also have determined a Quapaw's residence, position within the tribe, and duties in times of war and peace. It certainly regulated the choice of a mate. Because members of a clan were actually or considered to be close relatives, they had to look outside the clan for marriage partners. The Quapaws' clan and moiety memberships were patrilineal. This meant that children were members of their father's clan and moiety.

The village was the focus of Quapaw life. By the late 17th century, there were four of these. Tourima and Osotouy were both north of the Arkansas River, the former near the river's mouth and the latter 16 miles to the west; Tongigua was on the east bank of the Mississippi River, 11 miles north of the Arkansas; and Kappa was on the Mississippi's west side, 10 miles north of Tongigua.

Each village was a cluster of family dwellings and community structures. The rectangular dwellings were built of long poles driven into the ground, arched together at the top, and covered with cypress bark and cane mats. Each had a single entrance and a hole in the roof for ventilation. Inside were a fireplace in the center, a sunbaked clay floor, and sleeping platforms along the outer edges. In the summer, the Quapaws constructed outdoor sleeping platforms 15 to 20 feet above the ground to catch the cool breeze.

These family houses were situated around a central plaza. The site for friendly gatherings and community activities, the plaza contained at least two public buildings. One of these was similar in appearance to the family dwelling but large enough that several hundred Quapaws could assemble in it for tribal ceremonies and discussions. The other structure had a flat rectangular roof supported by four poles at the corners, open sides, and a carpet of fine rush mats. Headquarters for the local chief when the weather permitted, it was also the place where guests were entertained when they visited the village.

The governmental organization of the Downstream People reflected the division of the tribe into four separate villages. Each of the towns had a single chief who was responsible for making decisions affecting his community. This chief was not elected; the position was hereditary, usually passed on from father to son. The chief's decisions were always made after discussion with the tribal elders or a general council, the members of which were handpicked by the chief. The chiefs of the four different towns also probably consulted with each other on critical matters involving the whole tribe. Collective decisions were generally honored but never blindly accepted by each village.

When the Quapaws gathered in council and for ceremonies, each person's political importance determined where he or she sat. The chief, of course, was in front. Immediately behind him were the tribal elders as well as a group of younger men who had distinguished themselves in battle and who attended to the personal needs of the chief. Next were the rest of the men of the village. Behind them gathered the women and children. In the very rear, if included at all, were slaves. Members of other Indian tribes generally taken in battle, they occupied the lowest level of Quapaw social life and did not participate in the deliberations of the Downstream People.

The presence of slaves in all of the settlements reflected that the Quapaws were often at war. Having violently expelled the previous inhabitants of their Arkansas River homeland, the Qua-

paws were subject to frequent retaliatory raids from most of their neighbors, especially the warlike Chickasaws east of the Mississippi River. A chief could not declare war by himself. An open council met to consider the matter, and one of the chiefs or an orator explained the need for combat. When discussion ceased, the speaker held out a bundle of twigs. Every man who wanted to fight then announced his intention by taking one.

Preparation for the raid began the next morning. Symbolizing that the Quapaws would not be satisfied until enemy blood was shed, one of the warriors painted a club red; others carried it to the edge of enemy territory and placed it by a tree. On the tree they then carved two crossed arrows and painted these red as well. Meanwhile, the chief called another council, during which he invited allied tribes to join the expedition. Feasting, singing, and dancing followed. Members of the war party painted themselves red, acted out the imminent attack, and consulted their guardian spirits. The leader of the warriors fasted, purified his body, and painted it first black, then red. After an inspiring speech to his followers, he led them to encounter the enemy.

Following the battle, several of the youngest warriors would leave immediately to carry the news of victory or defeat to their villages. If the report was bad, the Quapaws would greet the returning party with weeping, cries of agony, and a period of mourning. But if the report was good, they would rejoice at the number of enemies killed and scalps and captives taken. The women determined whether the captives lived or died. Those who had lost a husband or son in the battle had the right to take one of the prisoners as a slave to replace the deceased. Captives who were not adopted were usually burned to death.

The Quapaws' elaborate rituals to prepare for war had much to do with their spiritual life. Central to their beliefs was *Wah-kon-tah*, the life force of the universe who had brought all things into existence. The Quapaws thought themselves related to clouds, rocks, animals, and all other things. They held equally in awe all that had life and all that did not, the seen and the unseen, the known and the unknown. In the heavenly world, the sun and the moon particularly were held in esteem, whereas in the earthly realm the serpent was of special importance.

Along with Wah-kon-tah, the Quapaws recognized other minor spirits: on earth, the water tortoise and two types of dwarfs; in the upper world, thunder people and special folk who walked the Milky Way. The Quapaws attributed

Farming the fertile land along the Mississippi River provided the early Quapaws with much of their food. River travel also linked them to neighboring tribes in a vast trade network.

The Quapaws' meals were served in clay bowls such as these or on oval wooden platters and were eaten with spoons made from buffalo horns.

the mysterious happenings of everyday life to the manipulations and activities of these spirits.

The Quapaws communicated with their deities through a special class of holy men, the *Wapinan*. They supervised ceremonies and religious rituals, advised tribal leaders on important issues, and performed feats of magic. They also selected the names of newborn children, which gave the Wapinan enormous influence over the tribe, because the Quapaws thought that a name could bring one success or failure. (They also attributed good and bad fortune to their individual guardian spirits.)

The Downstream People believed in an afterlife of either perpetual joy or torment. Close relatives buried the corpses in or just outside the family dwelling or next to the graves of others. If the body was buried outside the family dwelling, they frequently set small fires near the burial site to keep the corpse warm. If it was buried inside, the entire dwelling was set aflame, and

the family constructed a new house nearby. On or in the burial mound or sometimes atop upright stakes stuck into it, the family placed personal effects, gifts, and food to supply the needs of the deceased on the long journey to eternity. Relatives mourned for the departed, weeping and wailing at every sunrise and sunset until they calculated that the deceased had reached a bountiful hunting ground.

The Quapaws' war preparations and burial practices are good examples of their elaborate rituals and ceremonies, which were carried out for more everyday events as well. At meals, when guests were present, the host would paint himself red or black and serve food in two to four dishes, placing them first before the honored visitor. After the guest had eaten, the plates were passed to the person seated nearest to him, who ate his fill, and so on until all had eaten. The host replenished the dishes when necessary, but he himself never ate the food he served.

Tribal dances best illustrate the Quapaws' use of ritual. Their dances acknowledged and celebrated war, peace, religion, marriage, death, medicine, hunting, joy, and sensuality. The last were held secretly at night by the light of a large fire. Both men and women danced completely nude, coordinating their poses and gestures with songs that expressed their sexual desires.

Among the most elaborate was the dance of the *calumet*, which was performed to welcome visitors to the tribe. A calumet was a two-foot-long pipe stem made from a hollow reed, which was attached to a bowl of polished red stone adorned with colored feathers. Especially sacred to the Quapaws, the calumet was thought to derive from the sun the power to influence peace and war, life and death. The Quapaws cemented friendships with their Indian allies and distinguished guests by passing the calumet around for each person to smoke in turn.

Another important dance was the Busk, or Green Corn Dance. The Quapaws performed it in the late summer, just as the corn became ripe, to thank Wah-kon-tah for the anticipated harvest. The dance marked the end of a lengthy annual ceremony that celebrated the renewal of their most important crop as well as reaffirmed their Quapaw identity.

When the first Europeans arrived in the lower Arkansas River valley in the late 17th century, the Downstream People lived in harmony with their environment. Their social customs organized, explained, and gave meaning to their daily activities. Their economic system enabled them to fulfill their basic needs, and more. The Quapaws were a self-sufficient people, supported by their relationship with Wah-kon-tah, the natural environment, and each other. It was a self-sufficiency that the Europeans did not always appreciate or respect. ▲

When French explorers Jacques Marquette and Louis Jolliet, the first white men to encounter the Quapaws, arrived in their villages in 1673, the tribe prepared to fight them. The Quapaws put down their weapons when Marquette held out a calumet in a gesture of friendship and goodwill.

A
SOVEREIGN
PEOPLE

Seventeenth-century Europeans in North America had a variety of interests. These differed from time to time and place to place, but generally they were what could be called the three G's: God, glory, and gold. The continent "discovered" by Columbus seemed to offer untold opportunities to win God's favor and to gain personal fame and fortune.

France, Spain, and England waged a vigorous contest for control of North America's resources and people. The struggle initially focused on the Atlantic Coast, but by the late 17th century it had expanded into the interior of the continent. There, the competitors tried to form political and economic alliances with the native population. Because of the large number of Downstream People and the strategic location of their settlements on two major rivers, the Mississippi and the Arkansas, Europeans particularly sought their support.

The Quapaws had other options, but they elected to ally themselves with France. Several considerations ac-

counted for their decision, but the most obvious was that Frenchmen were the first Europeans to come among them. In July 1673, the noted explorers Jacques Marquette and Louis Jolliet reached Kappa, the northernmost Quapaw village, as they voyaged down the Mississippi River, which they thought would lead them to the Pacific Ocean. The Downstream People at first greeted them with bows and arrows drawn, but after Marquette offered them a calumet, the tribe welcomed the Europeans. They informed the Frenchmen that the Mississippi flowed into the Gulf of Mexico and that warlike tribes resided downriver. Discouraged by this information, Marquette and Jolliet abandoned their plans and turned back north to Canada.

Nearly a decade elapsed before another Frenchman reached the Quapaw villages. Looking for trade opportunities and hoping to confirm the actual course of the Mississippi River, Robert Cavelier, Sieur de La Salle, arrived at Kappa with a large party of explorers

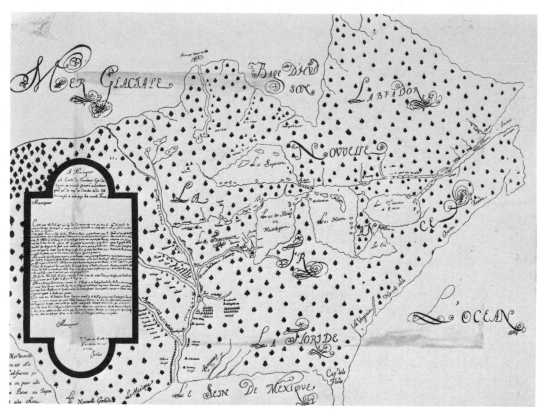

Jolliet drew this map of what is now the eastern United States and Canada based on his and Marquette's voyage down the Mississippi River in 1673. His original was lost during the expedition's return trip to Montreal, and he drew this one from memory in 1674.

in March 1682. Although they were initially suspicious, the Downstream People eventually received this expedition hospitably, providing shelter, firewood, and food. They even honored La Salle with a calumet dance. When the explorer had his men erect a cross and then a column on which the royal coat of arms was painted to claim the area for King Louis XIV, they danced again. As a demonstration of their respect, the dancers paused to rub the column with their hands, which they then passed over their own bodies.

From Kappa, La Salle and his men followed the river southward to the Quapaw villages of Tongigua and Tourima. The tribespeople there gave them information about their fourth village, Osotouy, which caused the French to estimate the total population of the Quapaws—perhaps too liberally—as 15,000 to 20,000. Three weeks after leaving Tourima, the explorer reached the mouth of the Mississippi River. There, on behalf of the king of France, La Salle took "possession" of Louisiana, a region he defined as all lands watered by the Mississippi River and its tributaries. La Salle then traveled back upriver, stopping only briefly at the Quapaw towns on his way to Quebec.

The tribespeople did not see La Salle again, although his influence lingered for years to come. Without the authority to do so, he gave his faithful associate Henri de Tonti a *seigniory* (a piece of land with commercial privileges), which was located on the Arkansas River and equal in size to the Quapaws' homeland. In 1684, Tonti established a post in the Quapaw village of Osotouy to watch for survivors of La Salle's ill-fated attempt to establish a French settlement on the coast of Texas. Eventually some refugees from the Texas settlement reached the post, where the Downstream People warmly welcomed

La Salle taking possession of Louisiana for the king of France in 1682, painted in the 19th century by J. N. Marchand. The column decorated with the royal coat of arms behind La Salle is similar to one the explorer erected in the Quapaw village of Kappa.

THE QUAPAWS IN THE 17TH CENTURY

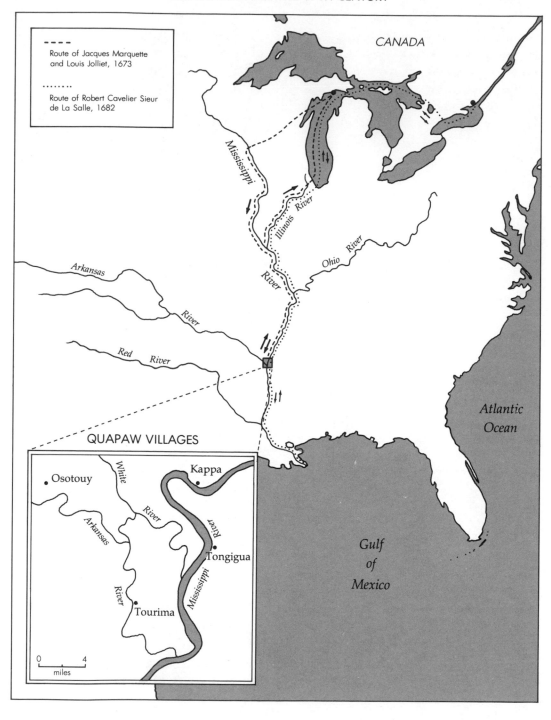

Route of Jacques Marquette and Louis Jolliet, 1673

Route of Robert Cavelier Sieur de La Salle, 1682

CANADA

Mississippi

Illinois River

Ohio River

Arkansas

River

Red River

Atlantic Ocean

QUAPAW VILLAGES

Osotouy

White

Kappa

Arkansas

River

River

Tongigua

River

Mississippi

Gulf of Mexico

Tourima

0 — 4
miles

them and even provided an escort for a portion of their journey north. La Salle was not among them; he was murdered at the hands of his own men in 1686.

In being so friendly to La Salle and his countrymen the Quapaws had not acted without self-interest. As early as 1680, the Downstream People had traveled to the Great Lakes region to trade with other Indians for French guns and knives, with which they could achieve dominance over enemy tribes. Hoping to trade for more of the Europeans' goods, the Quapaws believed that allying themselves with the French was to their advantage.

The strategy paid off when Tonti and his men initiated commerce with the Quapaws from the Osotouy post. There, the tribe eagerly exchanged buffalo, deer, and bear hides for a limited number of weapons and trinkets, such as beads and needles, which Europeans considered to be of little value but which were probably of spiritual significance to the Downstream People. Although Tonti was never able to develop permanent settlements on his seigniory, his men and their successors continued to search out the Quapaws for trading purposes. They also took hides, beaver pelts, bear grease, and hard buffalo fat in return for guns, ammunition, utensils, metal tools, alcohol, and luxury goods such as mirrors and buttons.

For the tribespeople the presence of any Frenchman in their villages was an implied promise that the coveted commerce would continue. When Catholic missionaries from the Seminary of Quebec toured their domain in 1699, therefore, the Quapaws urged them to send a priest to reside among them. Again their strategy worked; two years later Father Nicholas Foucault arrived to establish the first Christian mission in the region. On an irregular basis over the next six decades, four Catholic priests would serve the Downstream People but have little apparent impact upon their traditional spiritual life. The Indians evidently saw the missionaries more as potential connections to white traders than as religious leaders.

The Quapaws also elected to cast their lot with France because the French recognized the Quapaws' sovereignty as a people and a nation. With gifts, medals, and above all, respect, they acknowledged the Quapaws' authority over the region they occupied. Moreover, the French recognized their own dependence on the tribe. The Downstream People controlled access to the Arkansas River valley and could obstruct use of the Mississippi River, so the French knew they would need the Quapaws' help to realize their own colonial ambitions in the Mississippi Valley. It was as equals rather than as subjects, therefore, that the Quapaws embraced the French alliance.

In 1700, the successors of La Salle learned they could not take the alliance for granted. That year, English colonists from Charles Town in Carolina arrived among the Quapaws to establish a trad-

Pierre Le Moyne d'Iberville. D'Iberville's expeditions to North America in 1699, 1700, and 1702 helped France become the dominant European presence along the Mississippi River.

ing partnership. When the Downstream People expressed interest, the French tried to counteract this move by renewing their alliances with friendly Indians. Under the direction of explorer Pierre Le Moyne d'Iberville, they also reinforced their infant settlement at Biloxi on the Gulf of Mexico, established an administrative center nearby on Mobile Bay, and erected military posts where major rivers entered the Mississippi.

Assuming that it would give them greater access to European trade goods, the Quapaws welcomed this activity. But when the French efforts did not improve their trading, the Quapaws once again expressed interest in dealing with British agents. This demonstration of independence concerned the first governor of Louisiana, Jean Baptiste le Moyne de Bienville, who was the younger brother of Pierre Le Moyne d'Iberville. Bienville counted on the Downstream People to help contain the expansive Chickasaws, a tribe that occupied what is now western Tennessee and that was allied with the British. To solidify Quapaw loyalty, Bienville sent Lieutenant de la Boulaye with a company of 13 soldiers to establish a permanent military facility, Arkansas Post, near the tribal villages in the summer of 1721.

Thereafter the Downstream People seldom wavered from their alliance with France. They did not object in 1721 when a colony of French settlers vainly attempted to cultivate the Grand Prairie, which was adjacent to their settlements. The next year they permitted explorer Bernard de la Harpe to ascend the Arkansas River some 250 miles, even though the Quapaws feared that he might redirect the little commerce they enjoyed with French traders to tribes farther west. Eight years later, the Quapaws demonstrated their loyalty when they avenged the murder of missionary Father Paul du Poisson by taking scalps and prisoners from among the Yazoos and Koras to the south.

The Downstream People made their most significant demonstrations of allegiance in the 1730s, 1740s, and 1750s. During these decades France and England battled to determine who would control North America. Their clashes in the Mississippi Valley involving the Quapaws directly affected the outcome of this struggle. Between 1736 and 1739, Quapaws were among the 3,600 Indians and French who made 2 major but unsuccessful attacks upon the British-allied Chickasaws. In the 1740s, the governor of Louisiana asked the tribe to prevent French traders from using their villages as a starting point for the journey up the Arkansas River and over the Rocky Mountains to deal illegally with the Spanish at Santa Fe. The Quapaws promptly blocked this trade route, even though their initial cooperation had made it possible. The Quapaws continued to patronize French traders during the 1750s, although the British offered better goods at lower prices.

A cross and boulder today mark the spot where Pierre Le Moyne d'Iberville first landed on the coast of the Gulf of Mexico in 1699. At the request of the king of France, d'Iberville established the settlement of Biloxi, the first capital of French Louisiana, nearby.

For nearly a century of French allegiance, the Quapaws paid an enormous price. Especially devastating was the effect of the French on the tribe's population. By 1698, smallpox, a highly infectious disease unknown in North America before Europeans brought it to the continent, had reduced the Quapaws' warrior strength to 300 and their total population to approximately 1,200. Epidemic disease and warfare continued to diminish their ranks. By 1763, the Quapaw warriors numbered only 160, and the tribal population fewer than 700, down from the 15,000 to 20,000 La Salle had estimated only 80 years earlier.

French explorer Bernard de la Harpe, who was aided by the Quapaws when he led an expedition in 1722 to prove that the Arkansas River was deep enough for boats to navigate.

Because of their decreased population, the survivors of the Quapaw villages of Kappa and Tongigua merged in 1699 to create New Kappa, which was situated slightly south of Kappa's old location on the west bank of the Mississippi. A year later, the inhabitants of Tourima also joined their kin in New Kappa, leaving it and Osotouy the Quapaws' only settlements.

This consolidation had a direct effect on the Quapaws' government. Rather than having four chiefs acting together when tribal interests required it, the Quapaws came to look for leadership from a single, hereditary great chief. He was usually the traditional chief of Osotouy, the village that had suffered least from epidemic disease and stood nearest to Arkansas Post. The French officials encouraged—possibly even inaugurated—this new form of leadership, because they probably preferred to negotiate with only one person. They presented the great chief with a large medal to symbolize his authority, permitted him to distribute gifts allocated to the entire tribe, and assured him that they would deal with no other, lesser chief.

Equally disruptive to the Quapaws were economic changes resulting from the French alliance. Once predominantly farmers, the Downstream People so prized European manufactured goods that they came to spend more time on the hunt than in the field. The quest for buffalo and deer hides to trade with the French often left them in

THE

PRESENT STATE

OF THE

Country and *Inhabitants, Europeans* and
Indians,

OF

LOUISIANA,

On the North Continent of *America.*

By an *Officer* at *New Orleans* to his Friend at *Paris.*

CONTAINING

The Garrisons, Forts and Forces, Price of
all Manner of Provisions and Liquors, &c. also
an Account of their drunken lewd Lives, which
lead them to Excesses of Debauchery and Villany.

To which are added,

LETTERS from the Governor of that Province on
the Trade of the *French* and *English* with the Natives: Also
Proposals to them to put an End to their Traffick with the
English. Annual Presents to the Savages; a List of the
Country Goods, and those proper to be sent there, &c.
Translated from the *French* Originals, taken in the *Golden
Lyon* Prize, *Raffeaux,* Master, by the Hon. Capt. *Aylmer,*
Commander of His Majesty's Ship the *Portmahon,* and by
him sent to the *Admiralty Office.*

LONDON:

Printed for J. MILLAN, near *Whitehall.* 1744.
(Price One Shilling.

*This report on Louisiana in 1744 by a
French officer in New Orleans suggests proposals "to put an End to their [the Indian's]
Traffick with the English." Unlike other
tribes in Louisiana, the Quapaws were so
loyal to the French that they refused to deal
with English traders, even though the English often sold better goods at lower prices.*

want of the basic necessities of life,
making them even more dependent
upon the French for gifts and trade
goods. In short, they lost much of the
economic self-sufficiency that had char-

acterized their society before the French
arrived.

In two areas the Quapaws did resist
dramatic alteration of their earlier way
of life. Though friendly with Catholic
missionaries, the Quapaws' spiritual
life remained relatively unchanged by
them. Also, the Europeans contesting
for power in North America continued
to recognize the sovereignty of the
Downstream People. Despite the tribe's
decreasing population and increasing
economic dependency, the Europeans
perceived the Quapaws as a people of
influence and power.

Although overall their alliance with
the French did them more harm than
good, the Quapaws believed it was to
their benefit. By conscious choice, in
1682, they had cast their lot with La
Salle and his associates, and in later
years were proud that they had never
"soaked their hands in French blood,"
as Louisiana governor Louis Kerlerec
noted. Moreover, they were genuinely
distressed by France's defeat in the
French and Indian War (1754–61), in
which the French, with their Indian allies to the east, battled the English for
supremacy in North America. Losing
the war forced France to withdraw from
the continent. According to the Peace
of Paris of 1763, France ceded its pos-
sessions east of the Mississippi River to
the British. As compensation for
Spain's loss of East and West Florida
and its provinces in the Caribbean,
France also gave the area it had held
west of the river, including the Qua-

paws' homeland, to Spain. For the Downstream People, an era had come to an end.

Three years passed before Spain exercised any authority in Louisiana, though the new governor, Antonio de Ulloa, moved quickly to win the support and respect of the Quapaws.

Among other things, he rebuilt the facility at Arkansas Post on the Mississippi River, renamed it Fort Carlos, and assigned a new commandant and 50 soldiers to garrison it. In 1769, moreover, he distributed to the Quapaws 16 percent of the goods Spain had set aside as gifts for all the Indian tribes in Lou-

(continued on page 41)

French marine Jean-Bernard Bossu visiting the Quapaws. This engraving appeared in Bossu's 1777 memoirs of his travels in North America between 1751 and 1762. Its romanticized image of the Indians is typical of the period.

CREATIONS IN CLAY

Archaeologists have excavated a variety of ceramic vessels that were crafted by the Quapaws between the late 16th century, when the tribe migrated to the Arkansas River valley, and the late 17th century, when Europeans arrived in the area. Many of these vessels were made to serve everyday functions, such as cooking and storing food. But others with unusual shapes and decorations were created as objects of beauty to be used only during special ceremonies.

Quapaw women made their pottery from clay that they dug from the earth and mixed with water and finely ground pieces of shell from local streams. By hand, they kneaded this mixture into 6- to 7-foot-long rolls that they spiraled and molded into vessels, such as bowls and bottles. The Quapaws first set these objects in the shade to dry and then placed them in a bed of hot coals for firing. After the pottery had cooled, the surface of each piece was polished with smooth stones and water.

The Quapaws often decorated their pottery with three colors of paint: red, white, and either buff or black. On many works, they alternated these colors in horizontal or vertical stripes. But their most distinctive design was a pattern of interlocking curling lines, known today as the Quapaw swirl.

The tribe's most unusual and inventive ceramic creations are its teapots, a form created by no other North American Indians. Tea drinking was introduced by Europeans, and the Quapaws probably saw the teapots that belonged to French traders who visited their villages. Quapaw teapots have a round body with an opening at the top, a spout at one end, and a small knob at the other. The Quapaws often adapted this shape into the form of an animal. In these effigy teapots, the knob is transformed into the animal's head and the spout becomes its tail.

A rare human effigy bottle, measuring approximately 11 inches high and decorated with the Quapaw swirl.

The Quapaw swirl painted on this cat teapot, which measures about 12 inches from nose to tail, emphasizes the roundness of the animal's body.

An otter's back forms the base of this playful 7½-inch-long effigy teapot.

A 15-inch-long tadpole teapot with the feet of a frog and the mouth of a fish.

Red, white, and black paints create a distorted human face with one weeping eye on this 11-inch-long teapot.

The black paint on this 9-inch-long piece, which is unusually well preserved, was probably made from plants and is the least durable of the pigments used by the Quapaws.

A 12-inch-long teapot decorated with broad horizontal stripes of red and white.

The excellent condition of this bottle, which is about 11 inches high, suggests that it may have been used only for religious rituals.

An 8-inch-high bottle, whose neck is an effigy of an ear of corn.

The doughnut-shaped body of this 11-inch-high vessel suggests that it may have been a container for water. This shape provides a large surface area for evaporation, which keeps a liquid cool.

This 7-inch-long human head effigy is a unique interpretation of the teapot form: The back of the head is the teapot's base; the mouth, its opening; and the neck, its spout.

An 8½-inch-high fish effigy bottle. The Quapaws made red pigment by grinding hematite (iron ore) to a fine powder and mixing it with clay and water.

(continued from page 32)

isiana. Although Ulloa respected the sovereignty of the Quapaws, he obviously questioned their allegiance.

He had reason to do so. Presents and military posts aside, the Downstream People had reservations about any Spanish alliance. Spain traded the manufactured goods upon which the Quapaws had become dependent only at Fort Carlos, and at unusually high prices. Consequently, the tribespeople began to deal with British traders operating out of two posts, one on either side of the Mississippi River. By 1777, this commerce reached such proportions that both Great Chief Angaska of Osotouy and Chief Caiguaioataniga of Kappa had accepted the medals and flags the English presented to the chiefs to elicit their allegiance. Only the destruction of the British trading center on the west side of the river by Spanish-allied Indians induced the Quapaws to return to the store at Fort Carlos.

They did not come back any too soon. When the American colonials declared their independence from England in 1776, Spain first quietly, then three years later openly, supported the American Revolution (1776–83). The commandant of Fort Carlos recruited Quapaw warriors to scout British defenses among the English-allied Chickasaws. On April 16, 1783, he relied upon the tribe to help defend the post from a Chickasaw attack led by English trader James Colbert, who was married to a Chickasaw woman. The belated appearance of Chief Angaska and his war-

Don Joseph Vallier, who was the Spanish commander of Fort Carlos from 1787 to 1791.

riors prevented Colbert from making hostages of a former officer at Arkansas Post, the officer's wife, and two other white women.

The Chickasaws' attack on Fort Carlos came four months after England had recognized the independence of the United States in the Treaty of Paris of 1783. In this treaty, Great Britain ceded the land east of the Mississippi River to the United States and returned East and West Florida to Spain. No doubt Spanish officials believed that England's withdrawal would assure Spain's domination of the Mississippi Valley. It did not: The United States merely replaced England as Spain's competitor in the heart of the continent.

The Downstream People soon found that this new struggle made Spain prize their allegiance even more highly. Spanish officials negotiated for them a permanent peace with the Chickasaws in 1784. They also lavished presents on the Quapaws and expanded the selection of trade goods, especially liquor, available at Fort Carlos. Thereafter the tribespeople consumed so much of the fiery liquid that drunk-

enness and disorder within their towns became a problem. The Spaniards banned the liquor traffic after repeated incidents of violence. They feared this excessive drinking would reduce the Quapaws' military usefulness in discouraging Americans from moving into Spanish-owned territory west of the Mississippi.

For the Quapaws themselves, military readiness became more and more important for guarding their boundaries against the Osages. Of all the Indians living in Louisiana, the proud

Benjamin Franklin, John Jay, and John Adams sign the Treaty of Paris in 1783, in which England recognized the independence of the United States.

Osages were least inclined to bend to the Spanish will. Situated in what is now southwestern Missouri and northeastern Oklahoma, they raided as far south as Red River and as far north as the Missouri River, threatening even St. Louis.

Among Spanish-allied tribes, only the Quapaws seemed willing to challenge the warlike spirit of the Osages. In 1777, after a decade of conflict, the Osages petitioned Chief Angaska for peace, but hostilities resumed after the American Revolution. Promising guns and ammunition, the Spaniards encouraged the Downstream People to make war on their neighbors. They did so, but reluctantly, limiting their attacks to isolated, retaliatory raids in which, nevertheless, many of their warriors died. By 1793, no Quapaw hunter could venture safely into the Osages' country in search of game.

The will of the Downstream People to do battle for their Spanish allies weakened just as Louisiana faced its greatest challenge. In 1795, Spain signed the Treaty of San Lorenzo, ceding to the United States disputed lands on the east bank of the Mississippi River and acknowledging the right of American citizens to navigate the Mississippi freely. Spanish officials in New Orleans had hoped that the treaty would keep the restless American pioneers out of Louisiana, but they badly miscalculated. The number of Americans there actually increased. All of Spain's further efforts to contain the threat of American expansion failed, including plans for the Quapaws to harass the enemy. In 1801 Spain finally admitted defeat and ceded Louisiana back to France.

For the Quapaws, it was the end of another era. But the period of Spanish dominance had taken its toll. By 1800, there were fewer than 575 Quapaw men, women, and children. The inhabitants of New Kappa had separated into two smaller towns and, along with the population of Osotouy, moved to the south bank of the Arkansas River. A single chief presided over each village council, with Wah-pah-te-sah acting as principal chief of the entire tribe. The Quapaws continued to farm, but their economic well-being more than ever depended on trading hides for manufactured goods. Their ability to do battle with their enemies was now little more than a memory. Nevertheless, they remained the sovereigns of the lower Arkansas River valley, their position acknowledged by friend and foe. ▲

President Thomas Jefferson signing the documents of the Louisiana Purchase in 1803. Jefferson planned to relocate Indians living east of the Mississippi River into this vast territory in order to provide more land in the East for white settlers.

LOSS
OF
SOVEREIGNTY

Although the Quapaws would certainly have welcomed them, the French never returned to the Mississippi Valley. Initially, France had intended to make Louisiana a part of a new North American empire, but military reverses elsewhere made such plans impractical. Early in 1803, when U.S. president Thomas Jefferson offered to buy a part of the province in order to protect adjoining American settlements, Napoleon Bonaparte, emperor of France, suggested he purchase it all. The president hesitated, fearing that his office did not give him the authority. But seeing Louisiana as a place to relocate eastern Indians, he later swallowed his constitutional scruples and acquired it. Through the Louisiana Purchase the United States replaced France as the principal contact between the Downstream People and the white world.

After December 1803, the United States formally took control of Louisiana, which then comprised the lands west of the Mississippi that today make up the central third of the country. Just as both France and Spain had seen an allegiance with the Quapaws as crucial, American officials formulated policy to help make the tribe an ally. In May 1804, they had two barrels of tobacco and four of whiskey delivered to the tribal villages. The following year, the United States established a government trading post adjacent to the Quapaws' settlements. With these time-honored methods, the United States courted the Downstream People.

For a variety of reasons the tribespeople were not impressed. The trading post did not stock the goods they most desired, namely silverware, rifles, and scarlet cloth, and would not allow them to delay payment for merchandise. When Quapaw hunters chose to do business with independent traders, the government post closed. Also, American officials failed to favor the tribe with annual gifts, a European practice on which the tribal economy and government had come to depend. Equally dis-

The purchase of Louisiana almost doubled the size of the United States by extending its western border to the base of the Rocky Mountains. It also brought the Quapaw domain under the control of the U.S. government.

appointing, the Quapaws did not receive any direct communications from dignitaries in Washington, D.C., whereas they had received messages regularly from the leaders of France and Spain. In short, the United States denied the Quapaws an essential ingredient of any alliance: respect.

Initially, American officials cared little that they were losing friends in the Arkansas Valley. At least two developments changed that attitude. The first was President Jefferson's plan to encourage Indian tribes living east of the Mississippi River to withdraw to Louisiana. Among the first Indians this program affected were the Cherokees, some of whom emigrated west to new homes north of the Arkansas River. There, they encountered the Osages, who considered the newcomers intruders at best and deadly enemies at worst. Bloody conflicts ensued. The Downstream People then threatened to join the Osages to repel the invaders. With bloodshed at the end of the trail, few Cherokees wanted to relocate in the Osages' territory. This Indian war for the West jeopardized the removal policy cherished by federal officials.

The settlement of American pioneers in the Quapaws' domain also caused the United States to reassess its attitude toward the tribe. The fighting between the United States and England during the War of 1812 encouraged hundreds of settlers to find havens along the Arkansas River and especially in the Ouachita River valley farther south. An October 1815 report by the grand jury of Arkansas County stated that these frontier people had complained that the Quapaws and the Choctaws to the southeast were "daily in the habit of killing their cattle, hogs, and stealing horses, and committing personal abuse on the Inhabitants." Without being specific, they demanded that the local government find a resolution to their "problem."

More out of concern for the future of the Indian removal policy than for the well-being of the settlers, Missouri Territory governor William Clark did take action. He invited the Quapaw chiefs to meet with representatives of the Cherokees and Osages in St. Louis, the territorial capital, in the fall of 1816. For more than a decade the leadership of the tribe had anticipated receiving

such an invitation. To them it meant that finally Americans recognized their sovereignty as a nation. In November, they journeyed to St. Louis as directed. A Cherokee delegation accompanied them; the Osages declined to send any representatives.

In their first official negotiation with the United States, the Quapaw chiefs were accommodating, as they always had been under such circumstances. They did complain bitterly about the

The ceremony, held in St. Louis on March 9, 1804, marking the official transfer of the northern portion of the Louisiana Purchase to the United States. In 1812, St. Louis became the capital of Missouri Territory.

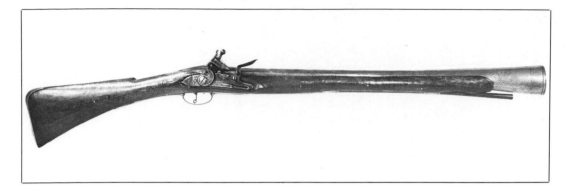

American rifles, such as this 1780 blunderbuss, were prized by the Quapaws. The rifle's name comes from Dutch words meaning ''thunder box'' and refers to the noise made when it is fired.

failure of the government to distribute gifts and about the intrusion of white settlers, but they expressed interest in adopting the agricultural improvements of the emigrant Cherokees. To obtain livestock, farming implements, and most importantly, an annuity (an annual payment of money or goods), the chiefs offered to cede more than one-half of their domain to the United States. Obviously, land was not as important to them as the proposed annuity, a thinly disguised substitute for the annual gifts that had been distributed by France and Spain.

Surprisingly, Governor Clark did not accept the Quapaws' offer. His superiors in Washington had instructed him not to negotiate with tribes who approached him wanting a payment of money in exchange for land cessions. Moreover, at the time, U.S. officials were not anxious to acquire Indian land for white settlers on the western frontier. These officials believed that a suf-

ficient amount of farmland existed in the East and also feared that the presence of white men in Indian country, especially along the Arkansas, could retard the removal of tribes from the East to the West.

The Quapaw chiefs accepted the rejection at St. Louis without bitterness. The negotiations had at least shown that the United States recognized the Quapaws' existence. They believed that perhaps they could yet persuade American officials to reinstitute the practice of making an annual distribution of gifts even if it cost possession of some hunting ground. The Downstream People did not have to wait long. Within two years their chiefs were called back to resume negotiations.

Three conditions had changed to permit the new discussions. First, white settlers in Arkansas County continued their campaign against the Quapaws, charging that it was unfair for only 160 Indians—the settlers' count was less than one-third of the actual Quapaw population—to control such a vast extent of land. Second, in July 1817, eastern Cherokees agreed to exchange a portion of their ancestral lands in the southern Appalachian Mountains for a tract in Arkansas where members of their tribe who had been removed could settle. Part of this tract was claimed by the Downstream People. Finally, the new secretary of war, John C. Calhoun, had no scruples against negotiating Indian land cessions in response to the demands of settlers who, living along the border of Spanish-owned Texas, would contribute to the defense of the republic. Thus, settler pressure, the desire to encourage removal of eastern In-

Map showing the boundaries set by the United States for several Indian tribes in 1816. Quapaw territory is labeled here as Arkansas, *a word derived from* Akansea, *the name given to the tribe by the French in the 17th century.*

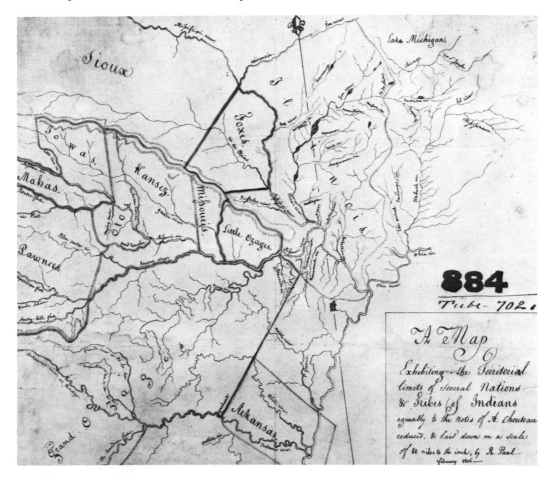

dians, and defense considerations led officials to ask the Quapaw chiefs back to St. Louis in August 1818.

Chief Heckaton headed the tribal delegation. A dedicated Quapaw patriot but not an especially forceful leader, he saw his principal objective as securing the annuity denied the Downstream People two years before. Governor Clark provided the delegates with lavish entertainment and gifts, includ-

General William Clark, governor of Missouri Territory, 1813–20. Hoping to sell the United States a portion of their homeland, the Quapaw chiefs met with Clark in St. Louis in 1816. However, the governor did not have the legal authority to accept their offer.

ing a military uniform for Heckaton's personal use, making the chief hopeful that this time he and his colleagues would succeed. They did, but at a considerable price.

After very little discussion, the chief and other members of the Quapaw delegation signed the Treaty of 1818, the tribe's first with the United States. The agreement secured the Downstream People a coveted perpetual annuity of $1,000 in goods, and a onetime bonus of $4,000 worth of manufactured items. In return, the tribe ceded all claims to the east bank of the Mississippi River and the north bank of the Arkansas River to the federal government. Even more important was its cession of a 43-million-acre tract bounded on the east by the Mississippi, on the north by the Arkansas and Canadian rivers, on the west by a line extending south from the headwaters of the Canadian, and on the south by Red River and an east-by-southeast line from the Red River raft (a logjam well known as a landmark) to the Mississippi.

The treaty did not leave the Quapaws landless, however. Within the ceded domain, the Quapaws reserved for themselves a tract of more than 1 million acres. It was bounded on the northeast by the Arkansas River, on the southwest by the Ouachita and Saline rivers, on the southeast by a line connecting Arkansas Post with the Ouachita, and on the northwest by a line running due northeast from the Saline to the city of Little Rock. The dimin-

ished reserve contained the three Quapaw villages near what is now the city
of Pine Bluff, Arkansas.

The significance of the Treaty of
1818 cannot be overestimated. For the
United States it spelled the success of
an increasingly popular removal policy,
because it cleared title to a tract of land
suitable for the resettlement of eastern
tribes. For the Downstream People it
meant a much reduced homeland, but,
ironically, in their eyes it also confirmed
their sovereignty and value as a people.
The United States had at last recognized
that the cooperation of the Quapaws
was necessary to make use of Louisiana
as the new home of eastern Indians. As
an ally of France and Spain, the Quapaws had sent warriors into battle; as
an ally of the United States, they provided territory. Heckaton and his colleagues saw no difference. Besides, the
Quapaws had obtained a perpetual annuity of greater value than the gifts that
had been bestowed annually by the two
European powers, and in return they
had relinquished nothing but hunting
territory. For the Quapaws, it was
hardly an even trade; they were con-
vinced they had gotten the best of the
bargain.

The white settlers in what had become the Arkansas Territory also
thought the Quapaws had outwitted
the government. "[W]hile we highly
approve the Benevolence and liberality
of the government in Making Provision
for that Peaceable and inoffensive tribe
of Indians," wrote one group of settlers

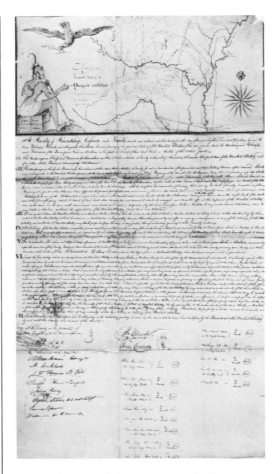

*In the Quapaws' first treaty with the United
States in 1818, the tribe ceded 43 million
acres of land in what is today Louisiana,
Arkansas, Oklahoma, and Texas.*

in a petition to Congress in 1818, "we
Deprocate [sic] the measure and Protest
against . . . unnecessarily lavishing
large Portions of Public and Private
Property on Savages while total indif-
ference or neglect is manifested to-
wards their fellow citizens." With no
thought given to the treaty and its legal

significance, other settlers demanded that the federal government acquire the remaining Quapaw lands.

These local attitudes endangered the Downstream People, threatening their most prized possession—their sovereignty. Equally dangerous was the growing disinterest of the very officials who had treated them as valued allies. The first $1,000 annuity went unpaid, and the government withdrew its subagent, the official it had stationed among the Quapaws to supervise fed-

eral programs in their domain. Moreover, the officials refused to protect tribal hunters from Osage attacks. Particularly disheartening for the Quapaws, the federal government accepted the results of an erroneous survey of the northwest boundary of their diminished reserve, which deprived them of another 800 square miles of territory.

Without the favor of the president, the "Great Father," as the Quapaws called him, Chief Heckaton and his people were virtually defenseless. Ru-

Map plotted by the General Land Office of the United States in 1821, showing the lands ceded by several tribes, including the Quapaws' 1818 cession.

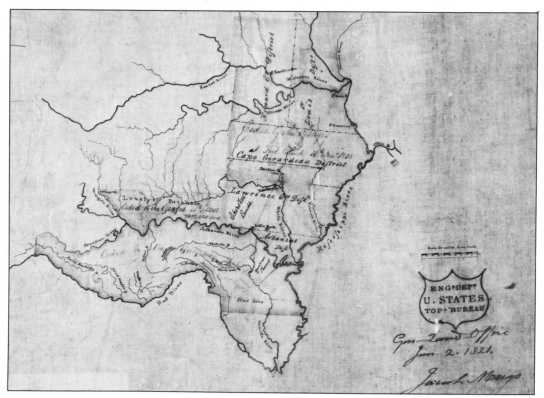

mors circulated in Arkansas that the Quapaws were willing to cede the remainder of their homeland and join the Caddos on Red River. Arkansas settlers demeaned the tribe as "a poor, indolent, miserable, remnant of a nation, insignificant and inconsiderable," according to a letter from Acting Governor Robert Crittenden to Secretary of War John C. Calhoun. In May and June 1824, without the authority to do so, Crittenden assembled the tribespeople and demanded they leave Arkansas. Heckaton vigorously objected, although he did agree to a further reduction of their reserve.

In November, Crittenden, this time with authority from Washington, D.C., reassembled the Downstream People at Harrington's, a white settlement near their villages. He announced that all previous discussions were now null and void and declared that the tribe would have to remove to an area in the northwest corner of the present-day state of Louisiana along Red River. Having expected only a request to cede a portion of their remaining lands, the Quapaws were stunned. Heckaton pleaded, "To leave my natal soil, and go among red men who are aliens to our race, is throwing us like outcasts upon the world. . . . Have mercy— send us not there." The governor was unimpressed. On Red River, he responded, the tribespeople would find a "manly and independent livelihood" in contrast to their "intoxicated . . . useless and effeminate" life in Arkansas.

Robert Crittenden who, as acting governor of Arkansas Territory, negotiated the Treaty of 1824 by which the Quapaws were forced to leave their Arkansas homeland and join the Caddo Indians living on Red River. In a letter dated September 13, 1823, Crittenden had assured Secretary of War John C. Calhoun that the Quapaw removal treaty would "rid the Government of them" forever.

Crittenden presented Heckaton and the other chiefs with a treaty that they had no real option but to accept. They signed it, maintaining the fiction for American officials, if not for themselves, that the two parties were equally sovereign. By the terms of the Treaty of 1824 the Quapaws ceded their diminished reserve and agreed to join the

Land Cessions of the Quapaws, 1818 and 1824

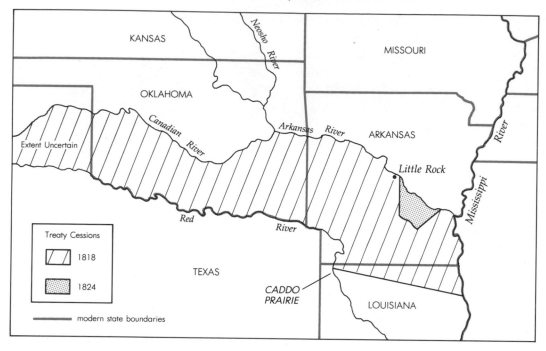

Caddos on Red River. In return, the government promised to pay $500 to each of the 4 chiefs, to distribute immediately $4,000 in merchandise, to provide food for 6 months, and to pay an annuity of $1,000 in coin for 11 years. However, there was no provision giving them a new reserve in exchange for the lands they surrendered, as there was in the treaties of removal signed by eastern tribes. The Downstream People were expected simply to merge themselves with the Caddos, losing their tribal identity as well as their ancestral home.

Removal to Red River did not occur until January 1826. The new governor of Arkansas Territory, George Izard, appointed Antoine Barraque to organ-

ize the emigration. A French trader who had done business with the Quapaws and who had once served in Napoleon's army, Barraque first prepared a tribal roll, which listed 455 individuals (158 men, 123 women, and 174 children). Then in groups of about 50 he started the tribespeople slowly toward Red River. By the middle of February, the first group of emigrants arrived on the north bank of the river in northwestern Louisiana. There they learned, unfortunately, that the Caddo chief preferred that they not settle among his people and absolutely refused to incorporate them into his tribe.

With the help of Barraque and the Caddo agent, the Quapaws crossed the river and established themselves in three villages on Caddo Prairie, just northwest of what is now Shreveport, Louisiana. They promptly planted their common fields with corn and scouted for new hunting grounds. But Red River flooded in May, washing away the young plants. The Quapaws replanted their fields, but the river flooded again in June. The food supplies and money that might have sustained them had been used up in the removal process. Completely impoverished, they starved. Sixty of them, mostly women and children, died. It is no wonder that after only six months in Louisiana approximately one-fourth of the tribe returned to their ancestral home. They were led by Sarasin, a chief of Quapaw-French descent elevated to authority by Arkansas officials.

Possibly conscience stricken, some residents and the local government of Arkansas Territory helped relieve the distress of the returned Quapaws. Governor Izard furnished them 500 bushels of corn. He also persuaded federal officials to pay to him one-fourth of a $2,000 emergency allotment, which he invested in farming tools and a fund for the purchase of land. These arrangements enabled Chief Sarasin's band to recover from starvation, establish settlements in isolated areas of their ceded homeland, cultivate small fields, and find jobs with white settlers as hunters or cotton pickers.

However timely the assistance, it could not prevent two tragic consequences. First, the ancient unity of the Downstream People was broken. Thereafter, even into modern times, factionalism would plague most aspects of tribal life. Second, the Quapaws were no longer an independent and self-sufficient people, much less a sovereign one. Their very survival depended on the annuity supplemented by disaster relief. Even federal officials seemed to recognize the tribe's disunity and loss of power, as they now recommended

George Izard, who, as governor of Arkansas Territory, planned the Quapaws' removal to Red River in 1825. When a band of destitute Quapaws returned to Arkansas Territory, Izard helped secure relief funds for them from the federal government.

After witnessing the poverty of the Quapaws, Territorial Governor John Pope attempted in 1832 to purchase land in Arkansas for the dispossessed Indians. His compassion led the Bureau of Indian Affairs' Stokes Commission to investigate the plight of the tribe.

that Sarasin's band merge with the Cherokees or Osages.

In the meantime, the Quapaws who had stayed on Red River struggled to overcome the disastrous first six months there. The federal government provided some relief with an emergency allocation. But the next spring the river once again flooded their fields. The Caddo agent recommended that the Quapaws relocate their villages 30

miles downstream, but it is not clear whether Heckaton and his people ever made the move. Throughout 1829 and 1830 small parties of Quapaws left Louisiana and rejoined their kin on the Arkansas River. By November 1830, virtually all had made the journey home.

Although reunification was a joyous event for the tribe, it did not ease the Quapaws' poverty and dispossession. Chief Heckaton tried to make these conditions known to the government through a personal visit to Washington in December 1830. To demonstrate that he could use federal money wisely, he gave his consent to spend nearly one-half of the tribe's annuity to finance educations for four young Quapaw men at the government-supported Choctaw Academy in Bluesprings, Kentucky. But neither his trip nor this concession won his cause much attention. Without government aid, the living conditions of the tribe deteriorated even further.

But when a new territorial governor, John Pope, took interest in their plight, so did officials in Washington. The three-member Stokes Commission, formed in 1832 to address the problems of all Indians west of the Mississippi River, finally put the Quapaws' case on its agenda. In May 1833, Commissioner John F. Schermerhorn, later notorious because of his negotiations for the removal of the Cherokees, assembled the Downstream People at New Gascony near Pine Bluff, Arkansas. After two days of discussions, he persuaded

Heckaton and the other Quapaw leaders to sign, however reluctantly, a third formal agreement with the United States.

The Treaty of 1833 was somewhat more realistic than earlier ones. Although it, too, required the Quapaws to remove from their Arkansas homeland, it assigned to the tribe 150 sections, or square miles, of land in Indian Territory (now Oklahoma) just west of the Missouri state line. The United States was to bear the expenses of removal and provide subsistence for one year after the emigration. The treaty contained provisions for supplying agricultural equipment and a farmer and blacksmith and allocated $1,000 per year for education. The treaty canceled earlier annual payments but authorized a new $2,000 annuity for 20 years. The Quapaws would have to leave their ancestral domain, but at least this time they would have an assigned homeland. The Treaty of 1833 appeared at last to be the U.S. government's guarantee that the Quapaws would retain their identity as a separate people. ▲

Spring River flows through the center of the Indian Territory reservation that the Quapaws settled in 1839.

A
DEPENDENT
PEOPLE

While the Quapaws still lived in Arkansas, local government played the largest role in shaping their destiny. Thereafter national Indian policy formed by the U.S. Congress would determine their future.

The official will of the government filtered down to the Quapaws through a mystifying bureaucratic structure. In 1824, Secretary of War John C. Calhoun created an agency, later known as the Bureau of Indian Affairs (BIA), to implement the government's policy. This agency communicated with the various tribes through regional offices, known as superintendencies, and local administrative centers known as agencies. Along with several other tribes, the Downstream People were under the jurisdiction first of a subagency and then later of the Quapaw Agency, which was attached at different times to the Western and Central superintendencies. Processed through this bureaucracy

and applied by a succession of different local agents, the government's Indian policy was often inconsistent and confused. Certainly it complicated both the Quapaws' removal to Indian Territory and their struggle for self-preservation there.

The U.S. Senate did not ratify the Treaty of 1833 until April 1834, 11 months after the Quapaws agreed to its terms. In the interval, the problems of the Quapaws worsened. Hoping to claim an unpaid annuity and fearing their impending removal to Indian Territory, some 300 tribespeople, nearly two-thirds of the Quapaw population, followed Chief Sarasin back to Red River. Upon arrival, they petitioned the government to permit them to remain among the Caddos, even though the Caddos remained hostile to them. The petition was denied, but the emigration demonstrated the depth of the factionalism that existed within the tribe.

In 1824, Secretary of War John C. Calhoun created the Bureau of Indian Affairs to implement Indian policy enacted by Congress.

Great Chief Heckaton and the 176 remaining Quapaws finally removed to their new reservation in September 1834. The agent in charge, Wharton Rector, led them to what is now the northeast corner of Oklahoma, to lands he took to be those assigned to the tribe in the recent treaty. Another agent issued to Heckaton's band the provisions promised by the government as well as livestock and farming equipment. They received the first $2,000 annuity with particular enthusiasm. The Quapaws built villages near the Neosho River and in the spring planted common fields with corn and pumpkins.

By late 1835, Heckaton's people were well enough established in their new homeland to encourage at least 100 of their kin on Red River to join them. The 200 remaining Red River Quapaws, who apparently composed one entire village, steadfastly refused to join those in Indian Territory. Instead, they crossed into Texas to join the small band of Cherokees led by Chief Bowles.

The Quapaw settlements in Indian Territory did not thrive for long. Rector had led Heckaton and his people to the wrong location, settling them in lands situated between reservations assigned to the Senecas and the Shawnees. When those two tribes merged into one, the commissioner of Indian affairs in Washington decided to combine their reservations. Because the Quapaws were living between the two, the government once again had to relocate the tribe.

In the spring of 1836, surveyors determined the boundaries of a new reserve. Three years later the government directed yet another removal, but this time they insisted that the Quapaws live in scattered individual homesteads rather than in traditional villages. This proved devastating to the tribe. Many abandoned the reservation, perpetuating the factionalism that would trouble the Downstream People throughout the 19th century.

THE QUAPAW AGENCY

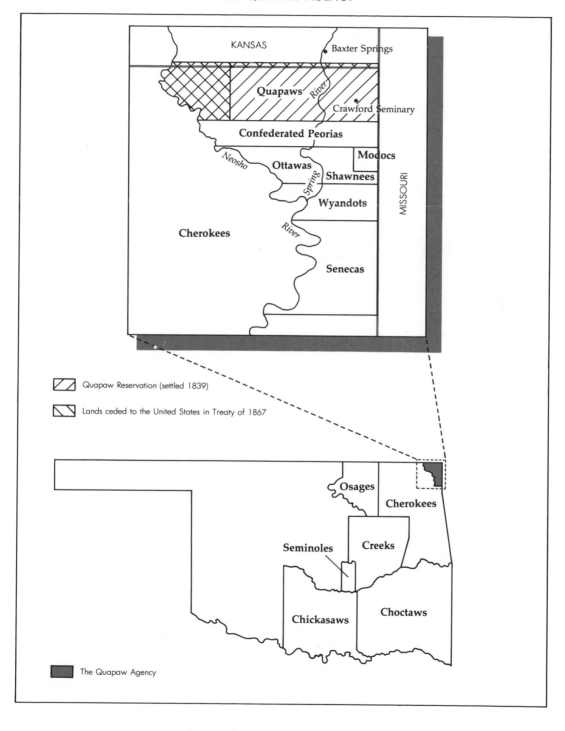

KANSAS

• Baxter Springs

Quapaws

Crawford Seminary

Confederated Peorias

Modocs

Neosho

Ottawas

Spring

Shawnees

MISSOURI

Wyandots

River

Cherokees

Senecas

Quapaw Reservation (settled 1839)

Lands ceded to the United States in Treaty of 1867

Osages

Cherokees

Seminoles

Creeks

Chickasaws

Choctaws

The Quapaw Agency

Approximately 100 Quapaws left to join their kin living in northeast Texas with the Cherokees, but the refuge they found was short lived. In July 1839, troops of the Republic of Texas, which had been established three years earlier when Texan colonists revolted against Mexico, drove them north across Red River. Rather than go to the reservation, the southern Quapaws elected to establish a village in the western part of the Choctaw nation in what is now southern Oklahoma. The Choctaws considered them intruders and evicted them. Wanderers again, in 1840 this faction of the Quapaws moved north across the Canadian River, where the Creek Indians permitted them to establish a village near what is now Holdenville, Oklahoma. By 1842, as many as 250 Quapaws resided at this location, which at least some of the tribespeople continued to occupy for the next 20 years.

As the Quapaws on the Canadian River adopted a traditional way of life, those on the reservation struggled to make the adjustments demanded by government policy. Not until 30 cabins, which had been promised in the 1833 treaty, were constructed in 1839 did they feel sufficiently secure to break individual fields and plant 100 acres of corn—a very slow start for a people once noted for their agriculture. They gradually increased both the acreage in cultivation and their yield until in 1850 there were 228 acres of farmland—approximately 1 acre per person—pro-

ducing 3,840 bushels of corn, lesser amounts of wheat, potatoes, and beans, and 5,000 melons. At least 1,000 fruit trees dotted the reservation landscape.

If farming or hunting ever failed to produce an adequate food supply, the Quapaws could always count on their $2,000 annuity. After 1840, these funds were paid in coin. In 1844, for example, 224 Quapaw men, women, and children received payments of $7.50 each. Although most spent their share on nonessential goods, such as cloth, guns, and whiskey, they considered the money absolutely vital to their economic survival.

It was also important socially. An annuity payment provided the occasion for all of the Downstream People, including those living on the Canadian River, to come together. At least 224 assembled in 1844; 264 in 1846; 221 in 1848; 271 in 1850; and as many as 314 in 1852. Much merrymaking always accompanied these affairs, but more important, they reestablished family and clan ties and provided a forum for the Quapaws' unique oral traditions.

The annual Busk, or Green Corn, festival, celebrating the ripening of their corn crop, also brought the Quapaw people together. In mid-August, the entire tribe gathered, each family bringing foodstuffs produced during the previous year. For two or three days they ate and danced, giving thanks to the Great Spirit for a plentiful harvest. Yet more was involved. The drums, the songs, the dances, the ceremonies, and

the rituals associated with the Busk recalled and renewed to each participant
his or her Quapaw heritage.

As these periodic gatherings of the
tribe illustrate, many ancient practices
had survived the trauma of removal
from the Quapaws' Arkansas homeland. Their social and political organization was among these. Although
government policy made traditional village life impossible, the tribe was still
divided into three basic social units,
which were reflected in its settlement
pattern. A chief presided over each
group, one chief being the hereditary
leader of the entire tribe. Heckaton held
this position until his death in 1842,
when he was succeeded by War-te-she,
who was probably Heckaton's son. The
three chiefs met in council as before to
make cooperatively those decisions affecting the entire tribe.

Thoughtful U.S. officials were not
surprised that the Quapaws retained
much of their cultural heritage. "Civilization," they assumed, required time
and, particularly, education. Thus they
were pleased that the leaders of the
Downstream People had an interest in
educating their youth. The experiences
of the first Quapaws to receive a formal
education, though, had not been encouraging. In the 1830s, Heckaton had
placed four young men at the Choctaw
Academy in Kentucky. Two left after 10
years: One rejoined the tribe; the other
settled among the Omahas. The one
who returned home could speak neither Quapaw nor English well. But

Methodist minister Samuel G. Patterson,
who founded the Crawford Seminary on the
Quapaw reservation in 1843. "This school
will be of lasting benefit to the Quapaw nation," wrote Agent B. B. R. Barker in 1844
to Commissioner of Indian Affairs Thomas
H. Crawford, after whom the institution
had been named.

Heckaton was even more distressed
with the second youth, who obviously
had learned "nothing," as the chief put
it, or "he would have known better
than to go up the Missouri to look for
his people."

But the Quapaws did not give up on
education, only education at the Choctaw Academy. In 1840, they demanded
a school near their own homes; if that
was not possible, they were willing to
return the annual payment of $1,000 for
education authorized by the Treaty of
1833. Samuel G. Patterson, a Methodist

minister from Missouri, opened the desired school and a mission station on the east bank of Spring River in 1843. The following year he named the facility Crawford Seminary in honor of the commissioner of Indian affairs. Financed by the educational annuity and Methodist church contributions, the school instructed as many as 28 students in the traditional American curriculum of the period until it closed in 1852.

The Quapaws, then led by Chief War-te-she, were at pains to find a replacement. They first looked to the Osage Manual Labor School in what is now St. Paul, Kansas. Run by Jesuits, members of an order of the Catholic church known for their scholarship, this institution had sent missionaries among the Downstream People since 1847 with great success. Perhaps because they reminded the tribe of its oral traditions and the Catholic missionaries of their Arkansas homeland, the school's priests were able to baptize as many as 280 Quapaws, including War-te-she, by 1855. Beginning in February 1853, Father John Schoenmakers admitted 24 Quapaw youngsters to the school, which for the next 17 years nurtured the tribespeople's interests in education.

Educating their students in distant Kansas was an admission by the Quapaws of their increasing dependence on elements of white culture and of the growing insufficiency of their own. In the 1850s, their recognition of cultural dependency was new; their economic dependency, however, had long been a given. The Downstream People realized that they depended totally on their annuity for the nonessential goods they wanted as well as for the unity they enjoyed with the Canadian River branch of the tribe. That need explained why the tribal leadership desperately sought a replacement for the $2,000 annuity when its 20-year period of payment ended in 1854.

To replace the coveted funds, Chief War-te-she proposed to sell part of the reservation to the U.S. government, something that most Indians did only at the point of the sword. But for the Quapaws the solution was hardly new; Heckaton had done the same thing in 1818. When the government turned down War-te-she's proposal in 1854, the chief was undaunted. He made a similar offer in 1857, and then again early in 1861. The government rejected those, too. Yet from War-te-she's point of view, the effort had not been useless. By 1859, the population on the reservation had increased to 350, up almost 80 people from a decade earlier. Unifying the Quapaws, even if only in the vain hope of receiving a cash payment for their reservation, had always been one of his principal objectives.

The primary reason the United States spurned War-te-she's offers was that they came during the crisis leading to the American Civil War (1861–65). The secession of the Southern states from the Union caused the government in Washington to withdraw its army and agents from the entire Indian Territory because, bordering on Spanish Texas, it would require too much manpower to protect. Left to their own devices, the Downstream People sought an alliance with the Confederacy, as did other tribes in the territory. In October 1861, Chiefs War-te-she and Ki-he-cah-te-da and two other Quapaw headmen signed a treaty of alliance with the Confederate government. Significantly, that agreement guaranteed to the tribe an annual distribution of goods valued at $2,000 for 20 years. It had required switching alliances, but the Quapaws were finally assured of receiving the treasured annuity.

If the Downstream People also embraced the Confederacy for reasons other than money, they did not demonstrate it in succeeding months. The part of the tribe residing on the Canadian River joined 7,000 Indians, who, led by the aged Creek Opothleyahola, refused to abandon the Washington, D.C., government. Throughout November and December 1861, these Quapaws united with Creeks and Seminoles to defend themselves heroically against attacks by troops of Confederate-allied Indians. Ultimately, the Union's Indian allies were forced to seek refuge in Kansas. As the South's armies surged closer to the assigned reservation of the Downstream People, Chief War-te-she and those still on the reserve in February 1862 also fled northward to join their kin and live as refugees near LeRoy, Kansas.

For the duration of the war, the reunited Quapaws suffered extreme privation and hardship, which included exposure to harsh weather conditions, sickness, and death. Some joined Union military expeditions into Indian Territory, but most devoted their energies to daily survival. Because of the cost of refugee relief, U.S. officials were anxious that they return to their reservation. On two different occasions the tribespeople actually left for Indian Territory, but Confederate forces south of Kansas forced them to turn back. After the conflict ended in June 1865, a small advance party of Quapaws finally reached the reserve.

The return of the remainder, however, awaited the negotiation of a formal peace between the United States and Confederate-allied Indians at Fort Smith, Arkansas, in September. The following month, nearly 4 years after they had been forced to flee, 265 Quapaws traveled back to their treaty lands led by Ki-he-cah-te-da, who had become the great chief following the death of War-te-she in January. It was a melancholy homecoming; the improvements made during their 30 years there now lay in utter ruins.

Despite the best efforts of the Quapaws, recovery was almost impossible. Crude shelters constructed along Spring River hardly kept out the winter weather. Lack of clothing caused them to suffer from exposure. Inadequate food supplies left them malnourished.

Following the Civil War, representatives of the U.S. government and Confederate-allied Indians convened at Fort Smith, Arkansas. The Quapaws were among several tribes that signed a peace treaty with the United States there on September 14, 1865.

Only rations provided by the agent saved them from starvation. Spring weather brought hope, but as had happened on Red River years before, crops planted in June 1866 were washed away by flooding. Thereafter the tribespeople subsisted wholly on roots and berries. Following the fall of the Confederacy, they had no annuity to cushion their distress.

As in the years immediately before the Civil War, securing an annual payment became the principal objective of the tribal leadership. Like his immedi-

ate predecessors, Chief Ki-he-cah-te-da proposed selling a portion of the reservation to the government. This time the offer was accepted.

Quapaw delegates negotiated a new treaty in Washington in February 1867. This agreement authorized the United States to buy the Kansas portion of their reserve and to purchase the western fourth of their land in Indian Territory on behalf of the Peoria Indians. Of the $30,000 proceeds from the 2 sales, the treaty stipulated that the government distribute $5,000 to the Quapaws upon ratification of the treaty by the Senate and invest the remainder in a trust fund at 5 percent interest. The interest earned was to be doled out in semi-annual *per capita* (individual) payments. The treaty also included other provisions for an educational fund and individual compensation for wartime losses, but those were of secondary importance to the Downstream People. Far more significant were the semi-annual payments, which would give them economic security as well as funds for luxury goods.

Although the United States soon took possession of the land granted them by the treaty, the Quapaws endured 2 additional years of deprivation before federal officials made the first $5,000 payment to them. Three more years passed before Congress appropriated the remaining $25,000. Contrary to the treaty terms, this money was not invested in a trust fund that would produce continual interest income. The government, with the consent of Chief Ki-he-cah-te-da and other headmen, instead paid the sum to the Quapaws per capita. The money for which the Downstream People sacrificed one-fourth of their reservation was quickly gone.

The government did abide by the Treaty of 1867 in its payment of a $1,000 annual stipend for education, a sum that had first been allocated in 1833. Un-

The Quapaw Industrial Boarding School was the principal educational institution serving the tribe from 1872 to 1901. Many people who became leaders of the Quapaws during the early 20th century were educated there.

til 1870, the Quapaws continued to send the money to the Osage Manual Labor School for their students enrolled there. The tribal leaders then withdrew their youngsters from the Kansas school upon the insistence of their agent, one of the Quakers who dominated the Central Superintendency during President Ulysses S. Grant's administration. Preferring a school with only Quaker teachers, the agent built a boarding school west of Spring River, which opened in 1872 with 50 students, less than half of whom were Quapaws.

Within 20 years, the school became a major institution, serving all of the tribes under the jurisdiction of the Quapaw Agency. Known as the Quapaw Industrial Boarding School, it eventually consisted of 13 buildings on a campus that also included a 160-acre demonstration farm. The school offered a strong academic curriculum through nine grades. Approximately 100 students were enrolled but there were seldom more than 20 Quapaws. To continue their education, some went to Indian boarding schools in Lawrence, Kansas, and Carlisle, Pennsylvania. These students became the next generation of Quapaw leaders.

The small number of Quapaws enrolled in school reflected a major decline in their population. After the entire proceeds of the land sale were distributed and all prospects of an annuity eliminated, many moved west to settle among the Osages. One of the first to go was Tallchief (Louis Angel),

Tallchief, also known as Louis Angel, was the last hereditary chief of the Quapaws. After he left the Quapaw reservation to live among the Osage Indians in 1875, the home band began to elect its chiefs.

who had become the hereditary chief following the death of Ki-he-cah-te-da in late 1874. By 1877, two-thirds of the tribe, representing two of the three traditional village units, had followed him. In 1883, the Quapaw home band, the tribespeople who continued to stay on the reservation, numbered no more than 38.

Government policy decisions partially explained this migration. Assuming that the Downstream People had more land than they needed, the Bureau of Indian Affairs thought of the Quapaw reservation first when it sought locations on which to resettle troublesome Indian groups. Such was the case with the Modocs in 1873, the Cheyennes and Arapahos in 1875, the Poncas in 1877, and the Tonkawas in 1884. Although none of these resettlements ever occurred, the negotiations for each panicked the Downstream People, causing more of them to move in with the Osages. The diminishing population only made the BIA more certain than ever that the tribe possessed land that it did not need.

The Quapaw home band disagreed, however. Because their hereditary leader now resided with the Osages, the home band elected new chiefs. Led first by John Hotel and then by Charley Quapaw, they moved to take advantage of the reservation's resources to

The Quapaws profited from the location of their reservation when cattle drivers, shown in an engraving from the 1870s, led their herds through their tribe's lands on their way to railroads in Kansas. Enterprising Quapaws charged the cattlemen for the right to use these trails.

Daniel Dyer, photographed here with his wife, served as the Quapaw agent from 1881 to 1884. He denounced the tribespeople as "generally worthless" after many Quapaws abandoned farming as a source of income in favor of collecting grazing fees from cattlemen.

overcome the tribe's past dependence on an annuity for the comforts, not to mention the basics, of life. After 1875, many Quapaws rented or leased reservation lands to non-Indian farmers in return for one-third of the crop. Within four years, this arrangement gave them a harvest five times greater than they had previously produced.

The growth of the cattle industry in the post–Civil War era also benefited the home band. One of the earliest trails

Texas cattlemen used to move their cattle to the origin of the railroad lines in Kansas passed through the Quapaw reservation. Drovers (cattle drivers) often grazed their herds on the tribe's excellent pastures prior to marketing them in Baxter Springs. Energetic Quapaws taxed the cattlemen for this privilege at the rate of 1 average steer for every 100 cattle that grazed there per month. Later, the railroad paid $200 annually for the right to establish loading pens on the reservation and 5 cents for each steer loaded. In 1884, the Cherokee Live Stock Company leased one-half of the tribal estate for $4,000 per year, paid per capita in quarterly installments. With this last arrangement, the Quapaws finally found a substitute for their lost annuities.

The home band's leasing of reservation property was in conflict with government policy, however. This policy initially had focused on the removal of eastern tribes to the western territories, in part so that federal officials could "protect" them from the corrupting influences of white society. The policy objective after the Civil War was to transform the Indians into "civilized" agriculturalists who appreciated Christianity, the value of individual labor, and the worth of private property. The collection of rent was considered uncivilized behavior. The Indian office, therefore, eventually voided the leases and exhorted the members of the Quapaw home band to become farmers rather than capitalists.

Although disappointed by the results, the Downstream People on the reservation learned much from their experience. They came to understand that the tribal estate was a valuable economic resource. They learned as well that traditional cultural habits could not always bring them luxuries, much less the necessities of life. Instead, these were best obtained through business transactions that only the educated could comprehend. Finally, they discovered that independence was not an option for Indians in their relations with the federal government or with the world at large. Treaties and notions of sovereignty aside, the Quapaws had become a dependent people. ▲

Stockbridge Indian A. W. Abrams became an adopted member of the Quapaw home band in 1887. Although he was never elected chief, Abrams's negotiation of the allotment of the Quapaw reservation made him one of the most influential leaders in the history of the tribe.

PRESERVATION
AND
ALLOTMENT

The Treaty of 1833 had bound the United States to recognize the Quapaws' title to their reservation only "as long as they shall exist as a nation or continue to reside thereon." With 80 percent of the Quapaws in the Osage country by 1880, many government officials legitimately questioned whether the tribe truly did "exist as a nation" and reside on its reservation. Fully aware of these doubts and that possession of a valuable reservation was in question, the leadership of the tribal minority moved boldly to confirm the rights of the Quapaws.

Relying on a practice that was common among American Indians, the home band elected to expand its membership by adopting individuals who would then come to reside on the reservation. The home band hoped to find the first candidates for adoption in Arkansas. In July 1883, Chief Charley Quapaw directed First Councilman Alphonsus Vallier to search there for Qua-

paw descendants to join them in Indian Territory.

In mid-August, Vallier arrived in the old homeland of the Downstream People. Older residents at Pine Bluff sent him to Abraham Dardenne, a well-known *métis*, or person of mixed Indian and non-Indian ancestry. Vallier explained his mission to Dardenne as well as to other families of Quapaw and French ancestry, namely the Rays, Imbeaus, and Hunts. In 1886, three years after Vallier extended the home band's invitation, Dardenne and Abraham Ray, another métis, settled their families on the tribal estate. Other métis soon followed.

The home band welcomed these newcomers, who doubled the reservation's population. The agent, however, questioned the right of the Arkansas Quapaws to remain on the reservation unless they were formally adopted by the chief and council and the adoption papers were approved by the government. At the local level this formality was accomplished immediately. The appropriate documents were then forwarded to Washington to the Bureau of Indian Affairs, which was now a part of the Department of the Interior. The petitions were approved by the secretary of the interior in March 1887.

The strengthened home band now began the systematic adoption of members of "homeless" Indian groups. Among these was a large contingent of Miamis, most of whom were the children or wives of white men. These included the Douthat, Gordon, and Carden families. Also adopted was a large party of New York Indians comprised in part of the families of James Newman, John Charters, and A. W. Abrams. When the flood of adoptions ceased in the fall of 1887, the home band had added well more than 100 persons to its population.

Although government officials had approved the home band's adoption of the Arkansas Quapaws, the commissioner of Indian affairs refused to sanction the adoption of homeless Indians. The BIA believed that the entire procedure was an attempt by white men to win control of the resources of the Quapaw reservation because many métis had so little Indian ancestry that they were considered white. The commissioner disapproved also because the adoptions had been made without the consent of the Quapaws living in the Osage country, still the majority of the tribe.

Since they had first left the home band in 1875, the Quapaws among the Osages had exhibited little interest in the activities on the reservation, preferring instead to follow a more traditional village life. By 1887, they had become concerned that the adoptions would dilute their rights to the Quapaw lands, which the home band discovered were of great value to non-Indians. That year Congress passed the General Allotment Act, also known as the Dawes Act, which authorized the breakup of Indian reservations and the allotment of 160-acre (one-fourth of a square mile) tracts to heads of families, 40-acre tracts to their children, and 80-acre tracts to single persons over 18 and orphan children under 18. Though the act did not directly affect the Quapaw reservation, the absentees could recognize that it was only a matter of time before their tribal lands would be allotted, and they feared they might not receive their share if they remained among the Osages. They also wanted part of the Quapaws' grazing receipts, which the Bureau of Indian Affairs would soon distribute per capita.

Therefore, the off-reservation Quapaws came home. Soon many, especially Peter Clabber, Francis Quapaw, and John Beaver, began to take active leadership roles. As their numbers increased, they began to wrest political control of the reservation away from the home band.

Although these new leaders opposed further adoptions of homeless

Indians, they at first made no effort to prevent the adoption of those who had already formally applied for it. The home band sent a delegation to Washington to persuade the commissioner of Indian affairs to reverse his decision not to sanction their homeless-Indian adoptions. Though not completely persuaded, he did order a field investigation of the matter, which led to his approval of an official Quapaw roll. The

Peter Clabber served as chief of the Quapaws from 1894 to 1926. Although he himself had lived among the Osage Indians for many years, Clabber ironically maintained in 1895 that Quapaws in Arkansas had "forfeited their rights" to allotments by not living on the Quapaw reservation.

commissioner planned to use this roll to pay out the grazing receipts that had accumulated in the agency's treasury.

Following a lengthy study of the reservation's population, the tribal agent prepared his roll in March 1889. It listed 121 Quapaw men, women, and children, including not only members of the home band but also the Osage absentees, Arkansas Quapaws, and homeless Indians who had been adopted into it. In Washington the roll was reduced to 116.

As soon as the roll was completed, adopted Quapaw A. W. Abrams insisted that it be "corrected." Initially a member of the Stockbridge tribe of eastern New York, Abrams had been educated in Kansas and had worked as a head sawyer in a lumber camp in Colorado and on the Pacific slope. He returned to Baxter Springs, Kansas, in 1887 and on July 6, at the age of 40, had been adopted into the Quapaw tribe by the home band. Intelligent, shrewd, and capable, he was soon employed by the tribal leadership as council clerk, conducting most of its correspondence and in time exerting a pervasive influence over its deliberations. Although the roll approved by Washington in May 1889 included Abrams and his family, he argued persuasively that the absence of some full-blooded Quapaws and deserving homeless Indians made it incomplete. In February 1890, federal officials again amended the roll, which now listed a total of 193 members of the tribe.

Joe Whitebird, who, with his wife, son, and two daughters, was among the 193 Quapaws listed on the tribal roll approved in February 1890.

Following three additional years of decisions by the government and appeals by Abrams, still another "final" roll was prepared. In 1893, the secretary of the interior declared that there were 215 Quapaws. Those counted included the home band, the absentees who had lived among the Osages, the Arkansas Quapaws, and virtually all of the homeless Indians who had applied for adoption. Because many of the latter had apparently paid a fee to have their Quapaw citizenship confirmed, Abrams's

reputation had become tarnished in Washington, though not within the tribe. The tribespeople recognized that by increasing the number of Quapaws, Abrams had ensured their vested rights to the reservation. For those whose names he had been responsible for adding to the roll, Abrams also guaranteed their entitlement to an allotment of land.

The allotment policy was widely supported within and outside the government, but the leaders of the Quapaws were concerned about some of its provisions. Specifically, Abrams and others contested the limitation of the size of individual allotments to 160 acres. Although allotments were restricted for 25 years from alienation—meaning they could not be sold—unallotted, or surplus, lands could be sold to the public. The Quapaw leaders, therefore, wanted the tribal reserve allotted in 200-acre tracts, which they believed would leave no surplus land for sale to non-Indians. Moreover, they wanted the Quapaw Agency incorporated into a county in Oklahoma Territory (formerly the western half of Indian Territory) and the Quapaws and other Indians of the agency declared citizens of the United States. They traveled to Washington as early as November 1889 to make this proposal.

The allotment bill supported by the Quapaws did not win approval from Congress, because it generated too much opposition. The Senecas objected to their agency being affiliated with distant Oklahoma Territory. Many powerful interests opposed the measure because it left little surplus land for sale to white farmers and would leave no tax base for local and state governments because allotments were to be nontaxable during the 25-year restricted period.

After four years of effort, Abrams and the council were bitterly disappointed by the continued reluctance of Congress to pass the bill. Assuming legislative approval was certain, many members of the tribe had already fenced in 200-acre allotments, built houses, and broken the prairie sod for cultivation. Indeed, Abrams himself had planted 500 acres of wheat. With 42,000 acres fenced and 10,000 being farmed, the Quapaws stood to suffer immense economic disaster because of the congressional rebuff. The council reasoned that dramatic and innovative action was required to protect the tribe's investment.

On March 23, 1893, in a general council meeting attended by all but four of the adult members of the tribe, the Quapaws unanimously agreed to allot their reservation without prior government approval. Signed by Chief John Medicine and 67 others, the measure authorized a 3-member committee to allot 200 acres to each enrolled member of the tribe. It also set aside 400 acres for a school and 10 acres (later increased to 40) for the use of the local Catholic church. Moreover, the measure stated that the allotment procedure would be

John Beaver, one of the many Quapaws who returned to the reservation in the late 1880s in order to receive an allotment of tribal land.

subject to the rules and regulations that the secretary of the interior and Congress might later prescribe so long as there was no decrease in the number of acres allotted.

The local agent forwarded a copy of the measure to the Bureau of Indian Affairs, with a diplomatic request from Abrams for its approval. Abrams also asked for three tract books with legal descriptions of the land in the area to facilitate the allotment committee's work. The agent sent along his endorsement of "the good work of the Quapaws," adding that "a grateful nation can not refuse the just demands of its wards." Washington officials delayed approval, but they did send the desired supplies.

In possession of the tract books, the allotment committee undertook the division of the tribal estate. The 200 acres selected by or for each of the enrolled members of the tribe were generally in a single location. The committee carefully entered the information into the tract books. Many Quapaws selected the 200 acres they had already fenced and improved, and a few family heads located the allotments of their children adjacent to their own. In this way, Abrams and his family, for example, obtained a block of 1,200 acres. By August 1893, the selection process was virtually completed.

Although the Downstream People believed that 200 acres to each enrolled Quapaw would take up the entire reserve, at least 12,000 acres of the tribal estate were left undivided. Had Congress accepted the committee's allotment proposal when it was first presented, Abrams would probably have agreed to the sale of this surplus land to non-Indians. Because Congress had not acted, he and his colleagues on the allotment committee, with the approval of the Quapaw council, assigned an additional 40-acre tract to each enrolled member of the tribe in March 1894. By the end of the year, the entire tribal domain had been allocated according to the roll approved earlier by the secretary of the interior.

After the allotment committee had finished its work, 25 Arkansas Quapaws living in the vicinity of Pine Bluff petitioned for adoption. The tribal agent brought the matter to the attention of the council. Unlike earlier peti-

John Quapaw, who was elected second chief of the tribe in 1894. He succeeded Peter Clabber as principal chief in 1927 but held that position for only two years.

tions from the Arkansas community, these were received with little interest.

At least two developments accounted for this reception. First, the tribal leadership had changed. In 1894, Peter Clabber, a former resident of the Osage country, was elected principal chief, and John Quapaw, a member of the home band, second chief. The shift of power to the absentees, who objected to adoptions, doomed the belated adoption petitions. Second, the division of the tribal domain was nearly completed. Any expansion of the roll would reduce the allotments already assigned. Thus, Clabber spoke for the majority when he noted that the 25 Arkansas Quapaws had "forfeited their rights" by not residing on the reservation, a curious comment from one who had himself long lived among the Osages.

By denying these adoption petitions, the Downstream People sought to preserve the work of Abrams and his allotment committee. Yet their division of the tribal estate had still not been officially sanctioned by Congress. As early as December 1893, Dennis Flynn, the delegate from Oklahoma Territory, had introduced legislation in Congress that would confirm the division of the reservation. But the commissioner of Indian affairs raised objections to that measure: He felt the size of individual allotments was too large, especially because the restrictions on this land prohibited state and local governments from collecting taxes on it. He preferred to reduce the number of restricted acres

Julia Stafford was 21 when she received her allotment in 1894. She later became wealthy when zinc and lead were found on her land.

per allotment to 80, leaving the rest subject to sale and taxation.

The commissioner's objections delayed but did not prevent the passage of legislation confirming the work of the Quapaw allotment committee. On March 2, 1895, Congress finally passed a law that accepted the committee's results "subject to revision, correction and approval by the Secretary of the Interior." Any Quapaw dissatisfied with his allotment could appeal to the secretary, who was also to issue fee-simple patents, which would grant each Quapaw the title to his or her allotment forever. The date of the patent would

An early 20th century gathering of Quapaw leaders wearing their traditional dress. Front row (left to right): John Beaver, Victor Griffin, the granddaughter of Tallchief, Tallchief, and Peter Clabber. Second row: Joe Whitebird, Silas Fire, Sigdah Tract, John Mohawk, Robert Lotson, John Crow, Francis Goodeagle, and his grandson.

mark the beginning of the 25-year pe-riod during which these allotments would be restricted from alienation and taxation.

Because the law gave a supervisory role to the secretary of the interior, in May 1895 the Bureau of Indian Affairs sent a special agent to evaluate the al-lotment process. There were few com-

plaints, although several Quapaws criticized Abrams's role in the proceed-ings, specifically his procurement of a huge tract of the best land for his family. Others, though, countered with en-dorsements of his character. "A. W. Abrams," wrote the commissioner of Indian affairs, "has been of great good to these Indians, and has done much toward improving their condition and preventing unscrupulous white men and others from defrauding them and getting control of much of their property."

Such testimony removed all doubt about the work of the allotment committee. Accordingly, the secretary of the interior approved the allotments made by Abrams and his colleagues. On September 26, 1896, he issued 234 restricted fee-simple patents to 200-acre tracts and on October 19, another 236 to 40-acre tracts. This action finalized the Quapaws' allotment process.

Allotment caused most Indian tribes to lose much of their land, because so-called surplus acres were sold to non-Indians. For the Quapaws, allotment did not mean dispossession, however. The entire estate was distributed only to enrolled members of the tribe. All that they had held in common before allotment they continued to hold as individuals.

Given the circumstances of the Downstream People a decade earlier, the preservation of the tribal estate was remarkable. In the early 1880s, the home band had numbered fewer than 40 people; white cattlemen and farmers had occupied their land; and government officials had sought to assign their reservation to other Indian groups. The Quapaws overcame these threats with a variety of creative strategies, among them the division of the reservation into tracts, which only Quapaws held by a legal title. For the Downstream People, allotment became a means not only of keeping their land but also of ensuring their perpetuation as a people. ▲

This great mound of gravel, or chat, in Picher, Oklahoma, was formed in the process of mining the deposits of lead and zinc discovered in the early 20th century on lands owned by Quapaw Indians.

BECOMING WARDS
OF THE
GOVERNMENT

The Downstream People embraced individual ownership of their tribal estate assuming it would give them greater control of their future. Congress saw it much the same way, although it charged federal officials with the responsibility of guarding the Quapaws' rights to their allotments for 25 years. During that time, the officials were also to educate the tribespeople to the advantages and dangers of the capitalistic economic system in the United States. Congress hoped the Quapaws would then be prepared to join the mainstream of American life as self-sufficient individuals. To the disappointment of both the tribe and the federal government, these expectations were never fully realized. The principal obstacle was unique: Many of the Quapaws struck it rich.

The source of their wealth was lead and zinc. Mining for these minerals in southwestern Missouri had begun well before the Civil War. In the early 1870s, engineers determined that the ore ex-

tended west into Kansas and southwest into Indian Territory, but not until 1897 was lead discovered on the Quapaw reservation. Forty to fifty thousand miners rushed to Quapaw lands when a rich field in Commerce, Oklahoma, opened in 1907. By 1914, nearly $5 million worth of lead and zinc concentrates had been mined. Over the next 25 years, 79 percent of the total value of the mineral output of the rich tristate (Missouri, Kansas, and Oklahoma) mining district came from the reservation of the Downstream People.

Before they could excavate these deposits, mine operators had to secure leases to use the land from the Quapaws to whom it had been allotted. Thanks to the influence of A. W. Abrams, Congress passed legislation in June 1897, that enabled the tribespeople to lease their land for 10 years without the approval of government officials so long as the lessor was not incapacitated "by reason of age or disability." Although meant to prepare the Quapaws for control of their land without any restrictions upon them, the legislation actually worked to their disadvantage. Unfamiliar with greed, they struck bargains that deprived them of the full value of their property.

The swindling took many forms. Some Quapaws leased their land for an inadequate royalty (a percentage of the mine operator's profits). Others sold valuable royalty assignments for a pittance. Many others leased for longer than the legal time limit or executed several overlapping leases. All were powerless to prevent malicious subleasing schemes by which the actual operator of a mine might pay a 25 percent royalty to an intermediary who would then give the Indian owner only 5 percent. A few were actually induced to sell their allotments despite the restrictions on alienation.

For a decade, government officials ignored these fraudulent transactions.

In this 1910 photograph Chief Peter Clabber (left) and Tallchief (right) pose beside a proclamation to the Quapaw people that had been signed by George Washington. Although Tallchief, the Quapaws' last hereditary chief, continued to live among the Osage Indians after allotment, he frequently visited the reservation.

But when an elderly Quapaw widow sold a royalty that was worth about $270 per month for $20 per month, they took note. The U.S. attorney general ruled in June 1906 that the government could intervene on her behalf because according to the terms of the 1897 law she was incapable of conducting her own business affairs. After the superintendent of the Quapaw Agency identified others similarly incapacitated, the secretary of the interior published a list of proposed regulations that extended the government's right to supervise Quapaw mining transactions.

The leadership of the Downstream People vigorously protested these regulations. Abrams rushed to Washington to argue the case, and Chief Clabber declared that the Quapaws had no need of a guardian to oversee their business matters. Their rebuttal was so effective that the commissioner of Indian affairs sent his personal secretary, R. G. Valentine, to the Quapaw Agency to assess whether government supervision was necessary. Valentine agreed with the Quapaws. They were, he said, "ready to be freed from the guardianship of the government," and any losses they suffered were worth "the cost of the experience."

Federal officials took Valentine, Clabber, and Abrams at their word. The secretary of the interior rescinded the proposed regulations. The Quapaws were once again on their own in dealing with mining speculators and operators. Too much evidence existed of widespread fraud in the mining district, however, for the government to ignore completely its responsibility to the Quapaws. The attorney general, therefore, assigned a special assistant, Paul Ewert, to the agency to see that the mine operators obeyed the law.

Arriving in Miami, Oklahoma, in December 1908, Ewert studied the situation for a year. He then concluded that "the leading businessmen of this community . . . have been guilty of . . . unlawful and fraudulent and conscienceless transactions." He proceeded to force the violators to "disgorge" approximately 9,000 acres of mineral lands secured by illegal deeds and to cancel unlawful agricultural and mining leases on nearly 30,000 acres.

In Washington, however, officials continued to pursue their general policy of "freeing" the Downstream People from supervision. Upon the recommendation of the secretary of the interior, in 1909 Congress authorized the government to remove the restrictions on all but 40 acres of adult Quapaws' allotments, if the owner of the land requested it. In 1912 and again in 1916 the secretary attempted unsuccessfully to win congressional approval to withdraw restrictions from adult allotments whether the Quapaws wanted the action or not.

Only a sensational case of graft caused government officials to reconsider their efforts to cut short the federal guardianship. Benjamin and See-sah Quapaw, a married couple with very

Benjamin Quapaw was perhaps the wealthiest member of the tribe when this photograph was taken in 1910. He later lost his fortune through bad investments.

traditional habits and perspectives, possessed two of the most profitable allotments. They granted control of their royalties and assets to Charles Goodeagle, an educated Quapaw, who invested their money in suspicious schemes in Baxter Springs, Kansas. Within 2 years, Goodeagle spent more than $120,000 of Mr. and Mrs. Quapaw's royalties and indebted them for $50,000. Legality aside, the immorality of the case forced the Bureau of Indian Affairs to take action.

In April 1917, the commissioner of Indian affairs placed under the close supervision of the government all Quapaws he deemed incompetent to conduct their own business affairs because of a lack of experience. These included children and uneducated Quapaws who had at least one Indian parent. The commissioner maintained he had this authority, citing both a new interpretation of the leasing act of 1897 and a 1915 decision of the Supreme Court. This ruling stated that the secretary of the interior had general supervision over the leasing of allotted Quapaw land, thus indicating that the government had responsibilities as a guardian that it previously had not exercised.

Subsequently, federal officials began to reevaluate existing leases on the allotments of incompetent Quapaws. They amended or even canceled the leases they deemed inequitable or fraudulent. They also assumed direct responsibility for the assets of individual Indians, ignoring all authority claimed by the local courts. Finally, in the federal courts, they sought and often won compensation for frauds perpetrated upon their Quapaw wards.

Despite the Quapaws' early opposition to government interference in their affairs, they welcomed the financial benefits of being wards of the federal government. They had already learned that there were advantages to the restrictions on their allotments, especially the nontaxable status of this land. Consequently, few Quapaws had elected to "free" themselves from the restrictions. Indeed, by 1920, only 36 living allottees had asked they be entirely removed. Fearing the expiration of the restrictions in 1921, Chief Clabber and the council urged Congress in 1912, 1917, and 1920 to continue the guardianship for another 25 years.

The commissioner of Indian affairs disagreed with the Quapaws only as to the extent of the supervision they still needed. He wanted the government to remain the guardian of only those Qua-

paws he found incapable of managing their own business affairs. A field investigation conducted in 1920–21 confirmed that of the 336 enrolled members of the tribe, only 31 original allottees and 31 heirs were actually legally incompetent. Some of these were under-aged or elderly, but others were deemed incompetent because they rejected the values of white Americans in favor of a more traditional Indian way of life. The property of these people encompassed 17,225 acres, or less than one-third of the land allotted in 1893.

Although the Quapaws hoped that the restrictions on all their allotments would be extended, Congress adopted

A gathering of Quapaw Indians in 1915.

the course recommended by the commissioner when the restrictions expired. Legislation passed in March 1921 extended the restrictions for 25 more years only on the lands owned by the 62 Quapaws identified by the field investigation. The law also authorized the secretary of the interior to prescribe terms and conditions of leases negotiated for those allotments and gave the state of Oklahoma the right to tax mineral production on this property so long as it did not become a mortgage.

With this legislation, Congress extended the federal guardianship for only 20 percent of the Quapaws. The rest, most of whom were less than one-half Indian and were Quapaw by adop-

tion, were no longer wards. They had neither the benefits nor disadvantages of government supervision. Many sold their land and then quickly assimilated into the white population of northeastern Oklahoma. Only on holiday occasions did they recall and celebrate their tribal heritage.

The Quapaws who remained wards of the government, however, retained a group identity, but one radically different from their ancestors'. Over the first 25 years of guardianship, they had benefited little from individual allotments, and their very possession of the land itself had been placed at risk. Moreover, many of their fellow tribal members whom they had once be-

A congregation of Quapaw converts to Catholicism on the grounds of St. Mary's of the Quapaws.

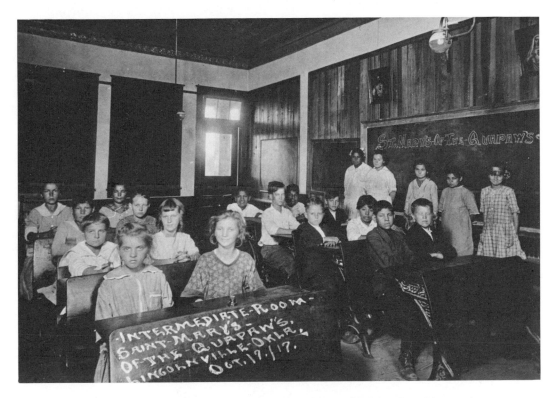

Class at St. Mary's of the Quapaws. Taught by the Sisters of Divine Providence of San Antonio, Texas, its courses were said to be "quite bookish . . . [and] pretty thorough."

friended and adopted had chosen to no longer live among them. These important shared experiences had helped to redefine what it meant to be a Quapaw.

One more positive experience that had an enormous influence over this new Quapaw identity was the flourishing of St. Mary's of the Quapaws. Established in 1894 by Father William Ketcham, St. Mary's included both a boarding school and a Catholic church, which were located on the land the allotment committee had designated for these purposes. By 1902 the school enrolled as many as 50 children in grades 1 through 9 and followed a curriculum described as "quite bookish . . . [and] pretty thorough." The church itself was equally successful. Father Ketcham reported in 1894 that with the exception of five or six, "all the Quapaws by blood are Catholic." Buffalo Calf was one of the exceptions. In a publication by the Bureau of Catholic Missions, he was reported to have said, "I do not care much for the white man's religion," yet he, too, agreed that the Catholic church "is our Church." By 1924, even the Quapaws' chief, Peter Clabber, had converted to Catholicism.

(continued on page 93)

THE PEYOTE RELIGION OF THE QUAPAW PEOPLE

Peyote, a non-habit-forming drug found in the buttons of the mescal cactus, has long been used as a religious sacrament by many of the Indians of North America. In Mexico, Indians performed peyote rituals at least as early as the 16th century. In the mid-1800s, the Apache, who traditionally had lived in southern Texas and northern Mexico, introduced the sacramental use of peyote to the Kiowas and the Comanches in southwestern Indian Territory (now Oklahoma). These tribes developed a peyote religion that integrated their traditional beliefs with the teachings of Christianity. After 1891, this religion and a version of it created by the Delaware and Caddo Indians in Indian Territory spread rapidly to Indian groups from the Great Lakes to the Rocky Mountains. Although the peyote religion was legally recognized as the Native American Church in 1918, U.S. officials and courts have long sought to deny devotees the right to use peyote in their services, a battle that continues among the tribes that still practice the religion today.

The peyote religion was introduced to the Downstream People in 1895 by John ("Moonhead") Wilson, an Indian of Delaware, Caddo, and French heritage. Wilson told the Quapaws that "Father Peyote" had transported him to the upper world. There he saw the empty grave of Christ and learned that the "Great Ruler" worked his will on earth through the sun, moon, stars, lightning, and thunder. Wilson also saw a road that led from the grave of Christ to the moon, the path that the suffering Savior had taken in his ascent. Father Peyote told Wilson to follow the road until the end of his life, when he would come into the actual presence of Christ.

Peyote worship as practiced by the Quapaws focused on the Big Moon. This was a permanent altar constructed of a U-shaped concrete slab that opened to the west. A straight west-to-east line through the middle of the altar represented the road that Wilson had seen in his revelation. This line pierced three cement hearts, known as the "Heart of the World," the "Sacred Heart of Christ," and the "Heart of Goodness," and intersected a north-to-south line to create a cross. Two mounds of ashes placed near the top of the altar represented the graves of Christ and of Wilson.

The altar was within a circular building, or "round house," which, like the altar, opened to the west. Services held here, usually on weekends, began in the evening and continued until noon the following day. Prior to the service, practitioners gathered inside a tent heated by red-hot rocks in order to sweat all the impurities out of their bodies. The worship service

John "Moonhead" Wilson, who introduced peyotism to the Quapaws in the late 19th century.

itself was conducted by eight men and consisted of singing accompanied by drums and rattles, praying, using peyote as a sacrament, and sharing candies and fruits.

The theology of the Peyote Road was distinctly different from the traditional beliefs of the Downstream People. Not only did it recognize the power of a single God and emphasize the person of Christ, it also stressed a personal rather than a communal relationship with the supreme deity. The peyote faith also called for upright behavior: Adherents were obligated to be honest, truthful, and generous; to preserve family bonds and earn their own livelihoods; and to avoid alcohol.

The Quapaws adopted peyotism in part because it helped them to conform to the prevailing standards of conduct of white Americans. It enabled them to adapt to cultural patterns that they had previously only appeared to accept. The peyote religion's emphasis on the individual also made it possible for the tribespeople to rationalize the great disparities of wealth that eventually developed as some of them became rich by leasing their land.

As individual Quapaws grew in wealth, Father Peyote grew in influence. During the 1920s, when lead and zinc mining on their lands brought some Quapaws an enormous amount of money, peyotism replaced Catholicism as the most popular religion among the tribespeople. In 1929, Victor Griffin, the high priest following the death of Wilson, was elected chief, a position he held until 1958. By that time, the mining had all but ceased and the monied Quapaws had died or spent their fortunes. Without the support of the wealthy, both Griffin's and the peyote religion's popularity within the tribe faded. A tribal revitalization movement in the 1960s, however, renewed interest in the religion's rituals, which are still practiced by a minority of Quapaws.

Quapaw practitioners of the peyote religion hold services in a circular building. Known as a round house, it contains the Big Moon, the altar that has always been the focus of peyote worship among the Quapaws.

(continued from page 89)

By the end of 1927, however, the school at St. Mary's had closed and the Quapaws' enthusiasm for Catholicism had dramatically declined because of the rising influence of the Peyote religion. A hybrid of traditional Indian beliefs and Christianity, peyotism appealed to the Quapaws because it was a religion that could easily accommodate old cultural patterns as well as new ones. One of the first converts was Victor Griffin. Young, intelligent, and resourceful, Griffin became the high priest of the new faith following the death of its founder John ("Moonhead") Wilson. Because of his support from the faithful with large incomes, Griffin was able to become a leader in the tribe.

The recent experiences of the tribal government also reinforced the group identity of the Quapaws. Since the 1880s, the council had consisted of first and second chiefs and three councilmen. Under the influence of A. W. Abrams, it had taken a bold step in allotting the tribal reservation without the initial approval of the federal government. Thereafter it met at least annually to consider various issues, ranging from the contract with the mission school to the extension of restrictions on allotments. These questions seldom concerned the adopted members of the tribe; thus, few of them ever participated in the deliberations of the council. Eventually, tribal government became the domain of only those whose restrictions had been extended. During the next 25 years of guardianship, this group would have to learn how to blend the old with the new if the Downstream People were to prosper as wards of the federal government. ▲

The grave site of John Beaver, one of the many Quapaws who became wealthy by leasing their allotments to mine operators. When he died in 1928, Beaver left an estate valued at more than one million dollars.

DISINTEGRATION
AND
REVITALIZATION

The federal government expected at last to prepare the Quapaws to manage their own affairs during the second 25-year guardianship (1921–46). Officials hoped the relationship would be more successful, cause less pain to the wards, and require less effort from the government than it had in the past. But the federal officials miscalculated once again. The immense value of the restricted allotments and the enormous revenue received from them strained the bond between ward and guardian.

From 1923 to 1943, mining royalties produced large, sustained incomes for Quapaw landowners. In that 20-year period, royalties totaled $14,689,599, peaking at $1,679,863 in 1926, dropping to $83,466 in 1933, and rising again to reach $969,901 in 1943. The number of persons receiving royalties varied from year to year, tending to increase as the estates of original allottees were divided among their heirs. In 1925, for example, 45 Quapaws received royalties; 10 years later, the number of recipients had dou-

bled. But the royalty income was not distributed equally among the allotment owners. Because some mines were more valuable than others, no more than about 10 families received the bulk of the royalty income. As a consequence, some individuals accumulated an astonishingly large amount of cash, many in excess of $200,000 and at least two approaching $500,000. By 1941, one Quapaw had more than $1 million.

Mine operators paid this money to the federal government, which credited it to the accounts of the appropriate allottees at the Quapaw Agency. The superintendent then disbursed it according to federal regulations. Most Quapaws to whom the money was credited, therefore, were forced to look to the superintendent for whatever funds they desired to spend. As a rule, each received a monthly cash allowance to meet day-to-day expenses, but large expenditures for appliances, repairs, vacations, and clothing required a pur-

Picher, Oklahoma, a town on the former Quapaw reservation, as it looked in 1925, the height of the zinc and lead mining boom.

chase order from the agency. If the superintendent deemed the Indian owner competent, however, he could pass on royalty income immediately without supervision.

Although the Quapaws were not masters of their own accounts, they were seldom without funds. If the superintendent approved, virtually any expenditure was possible. J. L. Suffecool, superintendent between 1924 and 1929, seldom disapproved, with predictable results: The Quapaws became enthusiastic spenders. In 1927, one spent $74,000, or five-sixths of his annual income; a couple, $73,000, or more than one-half of their income; another Quapaw, $30,000, or $7,000 more than his income. In the year preceding October 1, 1929, 30 to 35 Quapaws spent a total of $1.3 million.

Although a few Quapaws invested in homes, farms, barns, sheds, tools, and registered livestock, most of their money was spent frivolously. During Suffecool's superintendency, Quapaws paid out more than $262,000 for automobiles alone. Large amounts also went for clothing, tombstones, and va-

cations. Usually there was nothing to show for the disbursement. After spending $77,000 in a year, one Quapaw woman had assets of only $10,000 in cars and $3,400 in furniture.

The Bureau of Indian Affairs soon became aware of the spending orgy in the Quapaw Agency. After an investigation, the bureau dismissed Suffecool and his chief assistant. The Indian office directed subsequent superintendents to establish budgets for their wards, to refuse unauthorized purchase orders, and to prepare monthly statements of receipts and disbursements. These controls only partially curbed the spending spree. From 1928 to 1938, for instance, one Quapaw spent $233,543; $82,000 more than her income.

Although the Quapaws dissipated their incomes without thought for the future, they did not spend selfishly. Wealthy families hosted the entire tribe at annual powwows, funerals, memorial gatherings, and holiday celebrations, paying for all the food, prizes, and other incidental expenses. On these occasions, a family might entertain as many as 3,000 people at a total cost of perhaps $10,000. Furthermore, the homes of the wealthy were always open to visitors in need of a meal or a place to stay.

Though the BIA personnel had to bear part of the blame, the Downstream People were predominantly responsible for the rampant dissipation of their funds. With a recent history of abject poverty and a culture that had no concept of long-term saving, they valued money only for its ability to satisfy immediate desires. Their desires were many, and with funds at the agency available to satisfy them, the Quapaws were unwilling to stifle their appetite for goods. Moreover, they could not understand why they should be deprived of their wealth when non-Indians had unlimited access to their own money.

Though wealth for the Downstream People proved transient, it nevertheless profoundly altered many traditional cultural patterns. Those Quapaws who received royalties were set apart from their less affluent fellow tribespeople and were able to adapt more easily to the standards of white society. They increasingly accepted the teachings of Christianity and peyotism that emphasized personal religious responsibility. In financial matters as well, they came to pursue individual rather than common goals.

Family relationships were also affected. The Downstream People had always revered the family unit, especially its tradition of marital fidelity. The first generation of wealthy Quapaws retained this tradition, but the second wholly abandoned it. For the younger generation, divorce became the rule rather than the exception. Indeed, some Quapaws had as many as seven marriages, and some practiced bigamy. Couples would sometimes divorce and remarry, often more than once. One

The homes of one Quapaw woman before (left) and after (right) she received mining royalties.

Quapaw woman married the former husband of her sister, and one man married the former wife of his son.

This new pattern of divorce and remarriage left the family unit in shambles, shattering much of what remained of traditional Quapaw society. The clan system, leadership patterns, and other social customs became confused, if not meaningless, without the family. Already strained by the pressures of reservation life and the trauma of allotment, many of the remaining special qualities that had distinguished the Quapaw people disintegrated.

Federal officials expected their Quapaw wards to adopt the way of life of white Americans. The disintegration of their group identity and the instillment of individualistic values were part of the plan. They wanted the Quapaws to become self-sufficient individuals. But the agency's management of their money hardly helped to achieve that goal, and the way the federal government supervised the leasing of their mineral-rich lands actually hampered their ability to become more independent.

The right of the government to supervise the Quapaws' leases had been sustained in 1915 by the Supreme Court's decision. In the next decade, "supervision" became total, and sometimes imprudent, control. Two cases illustrate this point. In 1922, the secretary of the interior renewed the leases of the Eagle-Picher Company to seven different allotments. Because a competing firm had made a higher bid, the Qua-

paw owners objected and refused to sign the new leases. The same circumstances occurred in 1930 upon the renewal of the Skelton Lead and Zinc Company's lease on the Buffalo Calf allotment. In both cases, the superintendent signed on behalf of the Quapaws, and the courts upheld his argument that the Indians were unable to exercise independent judgment.

Despite this close government supervision, the federal guardianship did not prevent the growing individuality of the Quapaws. Pressures resulting from the disintegration of old traditions and the establishment of new ones were too strong. The Downstream People were developing a commitment to the pursuit of individual goals. This was apparent in the reaction of the tribal council to the Indian New Deal of the 1930s.

Following his inauguration in 1933, President Franklin D. Roosevelt appointed John Collier as commissioner of Indian affairs. Collier admired traditional Indian ways of life and believed that the communal orientation of tribes could help Indians achieve more productive and satisfying lives. He regretted his predecessors' attacks on Indian traditions, particularly the efforts that had been made to eliminate tribal ownership of land. The objective of his administration, therefore, became the preservation of the elements of traditional society that remained and the restoration of much that had been abandoned. He asked Senator Burton

K. Wheeler and Congressman Edgar Howard to introduce legislation into Congress to end further allotment of Indian land, return allotted as well as unallotted acres to tribal control, gather landless Indians on consolidated reservations, and establish tribal governments with corporate privileges.

Led by Chief Victor Griffin, the Quapaw council, in March 1934, rejected Collier's proposed measure "as a flagrant slap at Indian intelligence." The council believed that the new law would be unconstitutional because it infringed upon fee-simple patents and would deprive the Indians of their inheritance rights by returning previously allotted land to common ownership. The formation of new reservations, moreover, would force Indians to leave white communities of which many had been a part for 40 or more years. Finally, the proposed legislation would deprive the wealthy Quapaws of their mining royalties, distributing this income instead among all tribal members, including those who had sold their lands and/or no longer considered themselves Quapaws. The tribal council was more concerned about the individual sacrifice demanded by the measure than its communal advantages.

Expressed by other tribes as well, this attitude caused Congress to modify Collier's proposal drastically. In 1934, it finally passed instead the Indian Reorganization Act (IRA). The act ended allotment, banned unregulated sales of Indian lands, created a fund for federal

Victor Griffin, the last elected chief of the Quapaws, who led the tribe from 1929 to 1958.

loans for economic development of reservations, and established procedures by which tribal governments could become incorporated in order to transact business and hold property. But the IRA did not include Collier's provisions for tribal control of allotted land and the establishment of new reservations.

However, the measure exempted Indians in Oklahoma, including the Quapaws, although two years later Congress passed the Oklahoma Indian Welfare Act, extending the major benefits of the IRA to tribes within the state. The Downstream People ignored the law. They particularly resisted its plans for the reorganization of tribal government. The Quapaws preferred instead to continue with the chief and council system that reflected both their shared experiences as wards of the government as well as their emerging individuality.

As Commissioner Collier's original proposal had made clear, many of the interests of individual Quapaws continued to be in jeopardy throughout the 1930s. During the Great Depression, their right to their lands and incomes were threatened by mining companies, local and state authorities, and even federal officers. Annoyed as they were by federal regulations, the Downstream People recognized that their status as wards protected their individual interests. For that reason, they urged Congress to extend the restrictions on their allotted lands for another 25 years (1946–71). In July 1939, Congress granted the request on 89 tracts.

The relationship between the Downstream People and the federal government changed dramatically after World War II (1941–45). More than ever, officials were anxious to sever ties with their Indian wards. In 1946, Congress established the Indian Claims Commission to resolve all tribes' outstanding complaints against the government. The Quapaws were among the first to present their grievances.

Attorneys for the tribe asserted that the government's payment for land ceded under the treaties of 1818 and

1824 had been inadequate. For the more than 43 million acres relinquished in 1818, they requested compensation of $54,397,110.30. For the more than 1 million acres ceded in 1824, they asked for $1.25 per acre minus all payments already made under the treaty. Evidence filed in the case included hundreds of typewritten pages. The lawyers' briefs outlining their legal arguments were just as lengthy.

The commission made an initial decision in March 1951. It ruled against the Quapaws on their claims relating to the Treaty of 1818, but it did accept those concerning the Treaty of 1824. It awarded the Downstream People $987,092, minus the annuities received for the portion of their Arkansas homeland. Expecting compensation for the 1818 cession too, the attorneys for the Quapaws appealed the decision to the U.S. Court of Claims, but that court upheld the ruling of the Indian Claims Commission. When no further appeals were brought, the commission established $927,668.04 as the net amount due the Downstream People. In August 1954, Congress appropriated the money to fund the judgment.

The Indian Claims Commission award had an enormous impact on the Quapaws. When Chief Victor Griffin and the council attempted to limit distribution of the money only to those who were able to demonstrate one sixty-fourth or more Quapaw ancestry, individuals of very distant Quapaw relationship challenged the council's authority. Because no one could document how the traditional leadership had been selected or empowered to speak for the tribe, federal officials agreed that the Downstream People were without a recognized governing body. In August 1956, in Miami, Oklahoma, the Quapaw general council formally created a Business Committee made up of a chairman, vice-chairman, secretary-treasurer, and four councilmen, elected every two years to oversee tribal affairs. The tribespeople voted Robert A. Whitebird, a pure-blood Quapaw, into office as the first chairman.

Robert Whitebird was elected the first chairman of the Quapaw Business Committee in 1956. He retired in 1968.

The new tribal organization then took the steps necessary to secure payment of the commission award. In July 1959, Congress authorized the Business Committee to distribute the judgment moneys only to those living members of the tribe who were Quapaws by direct relationship rather than adoption and who could trace their ancestry to the allotment roll of 1890. The list of 1,199 Quapaws took 2 years to complete. In 1961, the government paid $946.41 to each of the Downstream People.

Though this sum was not huge, the payment of the Indian Claims Commission's judgment was of immense importance to the Quapaws, for it helped to revitalize their culture. The judgment brought together many young men and women of Quapaw ancestry, who for the first time learned of some of the traditions that had once distinguished the Downstream People. Unfortunately for the converts, most of those traditions had been lost. The few that survived became the focus of a cultural revival. Rituals associated with the burial of the dead were most often performed. Also, parents began to request Indian names for their children from Maud Supernaw, the elderly daughter of Tallchief, the last hereditary chief of the tribe.

Equally pivotal to the future of the tribe was the creation of the Business Committee itself. The formation of a new leadership structure had only been a matter of time. An invalid, Chief Grif-

Before her death in 1972, Maud Supernaw had been the spiritual leader of the Quapaws. The daughter of Tallchief, she bequeathed her father's sacred eagle feather fan and her position to Robert Whitebird.

fin had become physically incapable of leadership. Also, the source of his and the council's influence had virtually disappeared. Royalty income from mining totaled only $280,972 in 1956, just $12,424 in 1959, and nothing in 1960. When wealth had been widely distributed, Griffin and his colleagues represented many, if not all, of the Downstream People. With wealth limited to a few, they spoke only for a small minority.

Population changes also led to the necessity for a new form of tribal government. The Quapaws had numbered 236 in 1890; 350 in 1930; 600 in 1943; and 1,200 in 1961. The increase during Griffin's tenure as chief (1929–58) alone was 350 percent. By 1960, the majority of Quapaws had no ties to the few wealthy members of the tribe, and thus no ties to the traditional leadership. Furthermore, despite revitalization, many of the late additions to the tribal roll identified little with Quapaw heritage. This group welcomed the institution of a new leadership structure.

This change was supported as well by the federal government, whose role as the guardian of the Quapaws had decreased significantly. As the royalty payments diminished, so, too, did the need for government supervision. The majority of the Downstream People also now had little or nothing to do with those allotments still restricted by law. Federal officials encouraged a new tribal government, believing that it would give a voice to these members of the tribe while enabling the guardianship to end.

The Quapaw Business Committee responded admirably to the challenges of leadership. It took control of a 40-acre campground acquired by the previous council and made the annual powwow there a tribally organized venture. It also assumed responsibility for the 528 acres just south of Picher, Oklahoma, that the U.S. government had purchased in the name of the tribe in 1937. Initially leased to a local junior college for agricultural purposes, the committee made plans to transform it into an industrial park in 1975. The property remained largely undeveloped until the mid-1980s, however, when the tribe built a large and profitable bingo hall there.

The Business Committee under Robert Whitebird's leadership also refused termination—the federal government's policy inaugurated in the 1950s to sever all ties with the Indians—which had proved disastrous for many other tribes. In June 1970, the committee even prevailed on Congress to extend restrictions, which were due to expire in 1971, on 12,500 acres. Congress voted to continue the restrictions for 25 more years, or until 1996.

Although today only several hundred of the Downstream People participate in its annual meetings, the Business Committee is the principal cohesive force in the life of the tribe. Its gleaming new headquarters on the 40-acre tribal campground symbolizes that role. The magnitude of the current social welfare programs the committee operates, many under contract to the government, is a great source of tribal pride.

But the most visible display of the Quapaws' revitalization remains the annual powwow. More a social than a ceremonial occasion, it brings together all those who identify themselves as members of the tribe as well as other neighboring Indians for three days of visiting, feasting, singing, and dancing. In this atmosphere, many Quapaws rediscover, if only for a while, who they are—members of a people both ancient and modern, continually transformed by common experience. ▲

BIBLIOGRAPHY

Baird, W. David. *The Quapaw Indians: A History of the Downstream People.* Norman: University of Oklahoma Press, 1980.

———. *The Quapaw People.* Phoenix: Indian Tribal Series, 1975.

Din, Gilbert C., and Abraham P. Nasatir. *The Imperial Osages: Spanish-Indian Diplomacy in the Mississippi Valley.* Norman: University of Oklahoma Press, 1983.

Ford, James A. "Menard Site: The Quapaw Village of Osotouy on the Arkansas River." *Anthropological Papers of the American Museum of Natural History* 48, pt. 2 (1961): 133–191.

Nieberding, Velma S. *The History of Ottawa County.* Miami, OK: Walsworth, 1983.

———. *The Quapaws: Those Who Went Downstream.* Miami, OK: Dixons, 1976.

Oklahoma Indian Affairs Commission. *Ogaxpa.* Norman: University of Oklahoma Printing Services, 1977.

Westbrook, Kent C. *Legacy in Clay: Prehistoric Ceramic Art in Arkansas.* Little Rock: Rose Publishing Company, 1982.

Wilson, Charles Banks, ed. *Quapaw Agency Indians.* Miami, OK: privately printed, 1947.

THE QUAPAWS AT A GLANCE

TRIBE *Quapaw*

CULTURE AREA *Southeastern prairie*

GEOGRAPHY *Lower Arkansas River valley; now northeastern Oklahoma*

LINGUISTIC FAMILY *Southern Sioux*

CURRENT POPULATION *1,927*

FIRST CONTACT *Jacques Marquette and Louis Jolliet, French, 1673*

FEDERAL STATUS *recognized*

GLOSSARY

agent A person appointed by the Bureau of Indian Affairs to supervise U.S. government programs on a reservation and/or in a specific region; after 1908 the title *superintendent* replaced *agent*.

alienation The transfer of ownership of property from one party to another. Restrictions against alienation prohibited many Indians, including the Quapaws, from selling reservation land allotted to them for a prescribed period of time.

allotment U.S. policy, applied starting in 1887, to break up tribally owned reservations by assigning individual farms and ranches to Indians. Intended as much to discourage traditional communal activities as to encourage private farming and assimilate Indians into mainstream American life.

annuity Compensation for land and/or resources based on terms of a treaty or other agreement between the United States and an individual tribe; consisted of goods, services, and cash given to the tribe every year for a specified period.

clan A multigenerational group having a shared identity, organization, and property, based on belief in their descent from a common ancestor. Because clan members consider themselves closely related, marriage within a clan is strictly prohibited.

culture The learned behavior of human beings; non-biological, socially taught activities; the way of life of a given group of people.

Downstream People The Quapaws; derived from *Ugaxpa* (literally "those who drifted downstream"), the name given them by neighboring tribes in the late 15th century.

factionalism The division of one group into smaller groups or parties that are often argumentative and self-seeking.

fee simple A title, usually to land, that lasts forever and is passed on to the owner's heirs. Fee-simple patents were issued to the Quapaws by the secretary of the interior after the allotment of their reservation in 1895.

guardian A person, court, or government that legally manages and protects the rights and property of an individual or group of individuals considered incompetent to manage their own affairs.

hereditary Passed on from an ancestor. Throughout most of the Quapaws' history, the position of chief was hereditary.

incompetent An individual deemed incapable of managing his or her own affairs. The federal government judged many Indians, including some Quapaws, incompetent because they were underage, or elderly, or had chosen to follow a more traditional Indian way of life.

Indian Territory An area in the south central United States to which the U.S. government wanted to resettle Indians from other regions, especially the eastern states. In 1907, the territory became the state of Oklahoma.

patent A document conferring a right or privilege, especially the grant of legal title to land by a government to an individual. See *fee simple*.

patrilineal descent Relationship traced through the father's line.

prehistoric Anything that happened before written records existed for a given locality. In North America, anything earlier than the first contact with Europeans is considered to be prehistoric.

reservation, reserve A tract of land set aside by treaty for Indian occupation and use, often without the consent of the Indians themselves.

restrictions Prohibitions preventing Indians who held land titles from selling their land or using it in certain ways.

revitalization Rediscovery of and renewed interest in their earlier social institutions and traditions by members of a culture or ethnic group.

section One square mile (640 acres) of land. The basic unit of land surveys of the Quapaws' Arkansas homeland conducted by the U.S. government during the early 19th century.

seigniory Rights to control the use, especially for commercial purposes, of a specified land area in the French colonies. Seigniories were granted to individuals, usually by the authority of the king.

sovereignty Acknowledged political control of a nation or governmental unit over a region, leaving it free from external interference.

termination The removal of Indian tribes from federal government supervision and Indian lands from federal trust status. The policy was initiated by Congress during the presidencies of Harry S. Truman and Dwight D. Eisenhower.

territory The U.S. governmental status of a defined region that may become a state. Missouri, Arkansas, and Oklahoma were territories before they were granted statehood.

title Legal ownership, especially of property.

treaty A contract negotiated between representatives of the United States or another national government and one or more Indian tribes. Treaties dealt with the surrender of political independence, peaceful relations, land sales, boundaries, and related matters.

tribe A society consisting of several or many separate communities united by kinship, culture, and language, and such other social units as clans, religious organizations, and economic and political institutions. Tribes are generally characterized by economic and political equality and thus lack social classes and authoritative chiefs.

trust The relationship that exists between a guardian and a ward.

ward A person, usually underage or incompetent, who is placed under the supervision of a guardian.

INDEX

PICTURE CREDITS

W. DAVID BAIRD is the Howard A. White professor of history at Pepperdine University in Malibu, California. He holds a Ph.D. from the University of Oklahoma and was formerly chairman of the history department at Oklahoma State University. He is the author of *The Quapaw Indians: A History of the Downstream People* and *Peter Pitchlynn: Chief of the Choctaws* and the editor of *A Creek Warrior of the Confederacy: The Autobiography of Chief G. W. Grayson.*

FRANK W. PORTER III, general editor of INDIANS OF NORTH AMERICA, is director of the Chelsea House Foundation for American Indian Studies. He holds a B.A., M.A., and Ph.D. from the University of Maryland. He has done extensive research concerning the Indians of Maryland and Delaware and is the author of numerous articles on their history, archaeology, geography, and ethnography. He was formerly director of the Maryland Commission on Indian Affairs and American Indian Research and Resource Institute, Gettysburg, Pennsylvania, and he has received grants from the Delaware Humanities Forum, the Maryland Committee for the Humanities, the Ford Foundation, and the National Endowment for the Humanities, among others. Dr. Porter is the author of *The Bureau of Indian Affairs* in the Chelsea House KNOW YOUR GOVERNMENT series.